PRAISE FOR

Connecting Animals and Children in Early Childhood

"A beautifully written, beautifully illustrated, and succinct guide to children's connection with animals—its origins, its manifestations, its benefits, and how to promote it. Highly recommended."

—Howard Frumkin, MD, DrPH, Dean and Professor of Environmental and Occupational Health Sciences, University of Washington School of Public Health

"Selly's book is an outstanding, informative, and in. of our complex and potentially beneficial relationsh. animals. Well-written and illustrated, the book provides standing of the various ways humanity is enriched and enhanced by its connection with both wild and domesticated animals. The book is also realistic and practical, offering various pathways for particularly children to engage and learn from other life."

—Stephen R. Kellert, Professor Emeritus, Yale University, and author of *Birthright: People and Nature in the Modern World*

"What a wonderful resource for parents, grandparents, early childhood professionals, child care providers, and anyone caring for children. This delightful, enjoyable, and useful book is full of solid information about the magical relationship between children and animals."

—David Walsh, PhD, psychologist and author

"I enjoyed *Connecting Animals and Children in Early Childhood*. It is a well written resource that is easy to read, includes great pictures to share with children, and contains good information on how pets at home and in early education classrooms can help children learn about feelings. I would recommend *Connecting Animals and Children in Early Childhood* to anyone who brings a pet into a young child's life."

—Chad Dunkley, Chief Operating Officer, New Horizon Academy

"*Connecting Animals and Children in Early Childhood* is an engaging text that presents strong connections between background knowledge and practical, hands-on approaches to including animals in children's lives. Selly does an excellent job integrating research with practical ideas for supporting child development and the child-animal bond. Key aspects to child development such as social-emotional, cognitive, and physical development are discussed from a unique perspective that includes cultural, financial, and social justice considerations. In addition to providing practical tips for including animals in children's lives, Selly also presents information on how media influences human perception of animals and their behaviors. The passion that Selly has for animals and children is very clear when reading this text and should encourage all educators to consider how to include animals in their classrooms. This text is written with the concern for both children and animals and how animals can positively support child development. This may sound cliché, but I really mean it—this should be a must-read for any educator considering bringing an animal into the classroom as a pet. The section on planning and having meaningful interactions is especially crucial for early childhood educators to understand."

—Clarissa M. Uttley, PhD, Professor of Early Childhood Studies at Plymouth State University

"Even in the 21st century, the human brain remains powerfully attracted to animals. Patty Born Selly does a beautiful job showing us why that ancient, innate bond remains essential to the development of our children and our species. Selly's vision gives me joy and hope for the future. I hope all teachers and parents will take this book to heart."

—Meg Daley Olmert, author of *Made For Each Other: The Biology of the Human-Animal Bond* and Director of Research at Warrior Canine Connection, Inc.

"Patty Born Selly shows us how we can capitalize on children's innate connection with animals to create everyday opportunities to spur children's curiosity, engage children in learning that's meaningful, and connect children with other living creatures. This book is a powerful tool for any teacher who wants to bring more life into his or her teaching."

—Christy Merrick, Natural Start Coordinator, North American Association for Environmental Education

Connecting Animals and Children in Early Childhood

Other Redleaf books by Patty Born Selly

Early Childhood Activities for a Greener Earth

Connecting
Animals and Children
in Early Childhood

Patty Born Selly

Redleaf Press®
www.redleafpress.org
800-423-8309

Published by Redleaf Press
10 Yorkton Court
St. Paul, MN 55117
www.redleafpress.org

First edition 2014

Cover design by Ryan Scheife, Mayfly Design
Cover photograph by Sara Stenzel
Interior design by Percolator Graphic Design
Typeset in Cassia and Calluna Sans

Photographs on pages 8, 20, 26, 33, 37, 39, 46, 57, 72, 100 (bottom), 101, 103, 131, and 144 by Patty Born Selly
Photographs on pages 5, 7 (top), 10, 31, 32, 34, 35, 49, 61, 81, 93, 108, and 132 by Dani Porter Born
Photographs on pages 13, 14, 30, 62, 63, 97, 105, 109, 115 (top), and 141 by Sara Martin
Photographs on pages 19, 40, 42, 115 (bottom), 116, 118, 123, and 133 by Sinéad Carolan
Photographs on pages iii, 50, 54, 112, and 119 by Christine Muck
Photographs on pages 2 and 107 by Amy Lind

Photographs on pages 82 and 100 (top) by Dominic Wayne Selly
Photographs on pages 138 and 139 by Lisa Bigaouette
Photograph on page 7 (bottom) by Michelle Pryce
Photograph on page 17 by Dawn A. Flinn
Photograph on page 28 by Dynamic Graphics/Creatas/ Thinkstock
Photograph on page 29 by Ronda Bertsch
Photograph on page 41 by Bernadette Olvera
Photograph on page 51 by Rupak Nag
Photograph on page 55 by T. Martin
Photograph on page 57 by Mike Stoner
Photograph on page 59 by Sara Stenzel
Photograph on page 60 by Jeanne Erickson Cooley
Photograph on page 65 by Stockbyte/Stockbyte/ Thinkstock
Photograph on page 67 by Adam Crowley/Photodisc/ Thinkstock

Printed in the United States of America
21 20 19 18 17 16 15 14   1 2 3 4 5 6 7 8

Library of Congress Cataloging-in-Publication Data
Selly, Patty Born.
  Connecting animals and children in early childhood / Patty Born Selly.
    pages cm
  Summary: "This book presents the reasons why children's interactions and connections with animals are important, and it describes the valuable social-emotional development that results. It combines research, anecdotes, and a number of creative ideas that caregivers and educators can use to create authentic experiences for children" — Provided by publisher.
  Includes bibliographical references and index.
  ISBN 978-1-60554-156-3 (pbk.)
  ISBN 978-1-60554-353-6 (e-book)
  1. Education, Elementary—Activity programs. 2. Animals—Study and teaching (Elementary)— Activity programs. 3. Children and animals.   I. Title.
LB1592.S45 2014
372.21—dc23
                                                    2013040659

Printed on acid-free paper

To my family:
Dominic, Lucy, and Julian,
and Nina, Jamey, and Dragon

Contents

Acknowledgments

Mom, my earliest memories are filled with seeing you care for our pets, hearing you talk to the birds outside, and sensing the love you felt toward all animals. From you I learned how animals can fill up a heart with tenderness and joy. What a gift.

Dad, thanks for encouraging and believing in my writing since I could hold a pen.

Much to my delight, some of my heroes and sources of great inspiration were willing to talk with me about this project, hear my ideas, and welcome the addition of this book to the growing collection of work on children and animals: Tanya K. Bailey, MSW, LICSW, animal-assisted interaction program specialist at the University of Minnesota; Marc Bekoff, professor emeritus of Ecology and Evolutionary Biology, University of Colorado; Louise Chawla, professor at the University of Colorado; Stephen Kellert at Yale University; Gail F. Melson, professor emerita in the Department of Human Development and Family Studies at Purdue University; Gene Myers, professor at Huxley College of the Environment, Western Washington University; Meg Daley Olmert, author of *Made for Each Other*; Carol Saunders, PhD, Antioch University, New England; and Zoe Weil, Institute for Humane Education.

Throughout this work I have benefited greatly from the support and feedback of many colleagues, among them Peggy Ashbrook, author of *Science Is Simple*; David Becker, senior manager of learning experiences at the Chicago Zoological Society; Pete Cleary, Dodge Nature Preschool; Molly DePrekel; Lars Erdahl, longtime education director at the Minnesota Zoo; Ken Finch, Green Hearts Institute for Nature in Childhood; Seth Hayden, director of the Children's Country Day School; Cindy Hoisington, Pre-K senior associate, science curriculum and professional development at the Education Development Center in Waltham, Massachusetts; and Jan Welsh, education specialist at the Minnesota Department of Natural Resources.

I am grateful for the assistance of organizations including the Association of Zoos and Aquariums, the Children and Nature Network, the doctors and staff at Lake Harriet Veterinary in Minneapolis, the Minnesota Children and Nature Connection, the Minnesota Herpetological Society, the Monarch Lab at the University of Minnesota, the National Science Teachers Association, the National Association for the Education of Young Children, and the Humane Society of the United States. They provided clarity, verified accuracy, and offered critiques and professional expertise about a variety of issues addressed in this book.

Huge thanks to David Heath and the team at Redleaf Press for their meticulous work to make this book real, and to my brilliant editor Elena Fultz for her positive attitude, her gift for bringing coherence to this research and these ideas, and for her deadlines. Deep gratitude to the many parents, friends, and strangers who shared pictures and animal anecdotes with me. Dani Porter Born: If a picture is worth a thousand words, I give a million thanks to you. Thanks to Chris Gevara and Julie Schlangen of the Metropolitan State University Library for their constant assistance with obtaining needed resources during my research. Much love to my Monday night writing group, the creative, talented, and supportive group of mother-writers I am lucky to have in my life.

Heartfelt gratitude to the staff, teachers, students, classroom pets, and community of parents from Augsburg Park Montessori School, Children's Country Day School, Clara Barton Open School, Friends School of Minnesota, and Sunny Hollow Montessori. I applaud your recognition of the importance of animals in the lives of children. I am thankful to you for sharing anecdotes and photos with me and for letting me peek into the special world shared by children and animals.

Dominic, my love, once again you have consistently and cheerfully managed our home. You have fed, watered, and entertained our children and pets, and once again you've done everything in your power to support our family—and this work, and me—and I am deeply grateful to you. Thanks for tolerating so many late hours and fragmented weekends so I could write this book. I love you, always.

Lucy and Julian: every moment, you teach me what love is. You are my inspiration.

An Introduction to Animals and Children

My first zoo experience ended with me in tears. I stuck my chubby three-year-old finger through the chain-link fence surrounding the ostriches, and one of them nipped at my finger. I cried from the sheer surprise of it all. *This animal is real—and it just tried to eat me!* I must have thought. Whatever the ostrich's intentions, the lasting impression this incident made on me shaped my life. Rather than frightening me, the ostrich intrigued me. The interaction was one of several pivotal moments for me as a young child that ignited a world of interest in animals and the natural world. As a child and an adult, I have been fascinated by our interactions with the natural world, animals specifically.

This fascination led me down a career path that has been filled with opportunities to explore the connections humans have with the natural world. I've been a naturalist, wildlife rehabilitator, educational consultant, teacher trainer, and educator in K–12 schools and universities. I've also worked in nonformal settings, such as museums and nature centers, where I taught science and nature education for preschool and elementary-aged students, as well as teachers, parents, and families. And I helped hundreds of teachers successfully blend these topics with other disciplines in the classroom.

Recently, my focus has been on nature education and how teachers can be intentional and deliberate about environmental education in the early childhood classroom. While I was writing my book *Early Childhood Activities for a Greener Earth*, which concentrates on offering developmentally appropriate experiences about nature and the environment, I kept coming back to a central question: Where do animals fit into this picture? As I worked on that book, I discovered research that suggested meaningful encounters with animals in early childhood lead to stewardship ethics later in life. But that's not all. I also knew instinctively, as most of us do, that children *just need* animals in their lives. I have observed, as have many others, that something special seems to happen to children in the presence of animals. They are calmer, more curious, and more joyful. I wanted to be able to articulate why.

I continued to wonder, can children's natural love for—and curiosity about—animals be dovetailed into meaningful encounters with animals in the classroom? Are encounters with animals really that important? Do they have any real impact on children's development? Can early childhood educators provide children with meaningful connections with animals, even if they can't have animals in the classroom? What about animals at home? What can parents and other caregivers do to deepen and strengthen the strong bonds between their children and the family pets?

It's been my experience, and the research certainly bears it out, that animals can help children develop sensitivity to others, they can offer comfort, and they can even provide a safe sounding board for secrets and feelings that children don't share with adults. Animals provide opportunities for children to hone their social skills, practice caregiving and nurturing, and even to carefully explore issues of power and vulnerability.

Clearly, animals are important, and most adults recognize this. Children seem to know intuitively that different animals have different mannerisms and behavior, and require different treatment to evoke a response. Not only do animals ignite cognitive curiosity, but they also evoke emotional responses in children. Just think about the delight a child shows upon seeing a chipmunk or a family of ducklings paddling across a pond, or the sheer joy she expresses when a colorful butterfly flits past. A few wasps approaching a group of preschoolers having a picnic may elicit screams and panic. Present that same group of children with a fluffy white puppy, and the explosion of delight will be almost palpable. Many adults have anecdotal knowledge of the benefits that animals offer to children, or they seem to recognize intuitively the deep value in providing children with experiences involving animals. Perhaps these adults know from years of experience working with young children that animals are precious, exciting, and captivating for young children. Some educators are unable to articulate why they know animals are important for young children, but they "just know" that they are.

WHAT'S IN THIS BOOK

My hope in writing this book is to provide you with a bit of background. *Why* are animals so interesting and captivating for children, anyway? Why do children *want* animals in their lives? Perhaps more importantly, why do children *need* animals? What is significant about the perceptions and understandings that children today hold about animals? How does this impact their relationships with animals and with each other? And for the adult who wants to help strengthen the connections between children and animals, what are some ways to go about doing that? What brings an experience with animals beyond a one-time trip to a petting zoo that is quickly forgotten and turns it into a meaningful, authentic encounter that leaves a lasting positive impression on children?

Chapter 2 outlines some of the basic qualities shared by all animals that make them so appealing to children. Animals are special and important to so many of us, and I illustrate some of the many things that animals can inspire in us: feelings, actions, and beliefs that I believe ultimately make us better people.

Chapter 3 provides a look at the inner lives of young children and the development of certain key values, morals, and models for framing the world. The chapter also provides some examples of how animals impact children's development and growth: cognitive, social-emotional, interpersonal, and intrapersonal. The evidence is compelling that children-animal interactions provide clear benefits for children who have animals in their lives.

Chapter 4 provides an overview of animals in children's lives. Where do we find them? What kind of experiences are children having with animals? What factors influence the perceptions children form when it comes to animals? How do children demonstrate their understanding? From family pets and wild animals, to toys and stuffed animals, to clothing and media, animals are a central part of every child's landscape. This chapter explores some implications of children's experiences.

The concept of "authentic experiences" with animals is introduced in chapter 5. Authentic experiences are hands-on, supportive of children's understanding and learning, and respectful to both animals and people. The chapter also introduces some teachers and programs that have done amazing work to create deep, meaningful connections between children and animals.

The final chapter provides some real-life examples of how to bring animals into the classroom. It includes things to think about, suggestions for planning, ideas for finding the right pet, and resources for making your experience with a classroom pet meaningful, relevant, and joyful for children.

A NOTE ABOUT USAGE IN THIS BOOK

For the sake of clarity, I refer to nonhuman animals in this book simply as *animals*. Although humans certainly are animals as well, for the sake of brevity, I use the term *animals* to refer to all the other members of the animal kingdom—mammals, reptiles, insects, fish, amphibians, and birds—but not to humans. The reason for this is that, in their own usage, children exclude humans from their definitions of *animals*. In my research I have been primarily concerned with children's interest in, and relationship to, nonhuman animals.

The term *pets*, referring to domesticated animals in the care of humans, is often eschewed and replaced by the more recently accepted *companion animals*, since it doesn't imply ownership or possession. Many people also obtain animals specifically for their companionability. I use the terms interchangeably for the purposes of this book. A recent communication with the Association of Zoos and Aquariums informed me that the preferred parlance within that circle is *animals in the care of humans* instead of *exhibit animals* or the older *captive animals*. When I refer to animals in zoos, nature centers, or aquariums in this book, for brevity's sake I use the terms *exhibit animals*, or when necessary for context, *zoo/aquarium animals*.

When it comes to animals and our human relationship to them, words have meaning and power to influence our perceptions of animals. This book does not purport to tease out the moral implications of different terminology that humans use to describe animals. I provide these notes simply as food for thought for readers who wish to reflect on the nuances of our semantics about animals.

BRINGING CHILDREN AND ANIMALS TOGETHER

Maybe you're considering getting a classroom pet. Maybe you are a parent with a child who is an animal lover, and you hope to enrich her love. Maybe you are interested in the research on child development and animals, and you just want to learn more. Whatever your motivation for picking up this book, I thank you.

It is my vision and dream that every educator and parent who works with children will recognize and value the special love that children feel for animals and that more adults will nurture that love. Nurturing that love will mean that more children are honored and supported. The growing awareness of the importance of animals in the lives of children will lead to more animals being loved by children, treasured not just for what they can bring to children's lives but simply for what they are.

Why Are Children So Interested in Animals, Anyway?

Ava has loved cats since she was old enough to turn her head and watch the family cat strut across the room. Now that she's six, she even knows when her pet's birthday is, often makes cards and gifts for him, and runs to greet him each day when she arrives home from school.

Matthew watches out the classroom window at his preschool each morning, waiting for "his" squirrel to hop by.

Jasmine loves horses and ponies, and although she's never seen one in real life, her teacher says she's almost obsessed with them—she draws pictures of them and selects books about them, and her favorite toy is a stuffed horse.

Whatever form a child's love for animals takes, it's obvious that animals are very special to children. Some children are more forthcoming about their love than others. Some children have lots of favorites, and others limit their love to just one or two. What seems to be universally true is that just about any child you ask will be able to tell you something he loves about animals. Ask a shy child what her favorite animal is, and she'll open up right away. Children love to tell stories about their own pets, animals they've seen in the wild, special memories of the zoo, and other meaningful events. This alone tells us something basic and simple: *animals are important and special to children*.

Many people intuitively understand but perhaps have never heard of the "biophilia hypothesis," the idea, put forward by biologist Edward O. Wilson in 1984, that humans have a natural affinity for other living things—plants, animals, and the natural environment. According to Wilson, because we are alive, we humans all share an innate need to associate with other living creatures. In recent years, many early childhood educators have recognized

this need and are trying to embrace this philosophy in their centers by offering natural materials in the classroom (such as plants and planted flowers), creating nature-based play areas, and providing plenty of outdoor time for children. The biophilia hypothesis supports the idea that children can thrive when allowed extended periods of time in natural settings. In *Building for Life: Designing and Understanding the Human-Nature Connection*, Stephen R. Kellert observes that a number of studies have shown that children's academic growth, behavior, and stress levels improved when they interacted with their living environment. Children's cooperation with others, creativity, and physical health also increased. When an educator recognizes biophilia by including other forms of life in her model of child development, one might say she is following a biocentric approach.

But having a biocentric approach to child development means more than just providing children with spaces to run and play in nature. It can also include opportunities for children to connect with living animals. Animals offer a unique window into another world. Children's relationships with animals are special, rich with meaning, and supportive of children's development. Focusing on children's relationships with animals encourages and expands children's affinity for living things.

Children's innate love for animals seems to be universal. While most adults tend to place value on animals based on their relationship to humans (for example, valuing them for companionship, food, or products, such as leather or wool), young children seem to value animals simply because they *are*. This is called *intrinsic* value. Many children recognize the intrinsic value of animals not because of what they do for us, what they give to us, or how they help us, but simply because they are living creatures. Children don't consider the elements and nuances of their relationships to and love for animals. Most simply love animals without question or analysis. Ask a group of preschoolers what they think of animals, and they'll express that disliking animals is simply "wrong," that caring for animals is just a natural, normal way of being.

While the reasons that adults and children alike find animals so exciting and captivating may be rooted in our biology, psychology, or something else, there's no denying animals' widespread appeal. But what *specifically* about the animals makes them so special to children? Why are children universally drawn to animals?

Animals have many common characteristics that appeal to children. But how children perceive animals and their characteristics is influenced by many factors: cultural and family beliefs and values; media such as books,

television, and movies; personal experiences; and exposure to animals in settings such as nature, zoos, the classroom, and at home. Some animals possess certain qualities, but others do not, and these qualities may appeal to some children but not to others. For example, a child may deeply love frogs but for reasons different from any discussed below. Each child is unique, and just as we know that there are multiple intelligences and multiple ways to learn, we recognize that there are also multiple ways that animals find their way into the hearts and minds of children. Here are some of the ways that this happens.

PART OF THE FAMILY

Many children are exposed to animals for the first time through a pet at home. Babies smile and giggle as they watch pets with rapt attention. Growing up in the same household, a child may well develop strong bonds with a pet or other animals they interact with. A child can feel deep love for a classroom pet, a neighbor's cat, and even the neighborhood animals they see and encounter outside. Children who interact regularly with certain animals may appreciate them because they are part of the children's everyday, familiar social world. The love a young child feels for the family pet may go well beyond a simple enjoyment of playtime and cuddle time. A child's love may include, for example, a sense that the pet is "one of the family."

IT'S A ZOO OUT THERE: SENSORY STIMULATION

Many young children's interest in animals is sparked by exposure to the sensory stimulation animals offer. The many species in the animal world have an incredible variety of shapes, sizes, colors, textures, sounds, and even smells. Animals offer constant novelty for the senses. This is one reason that zoos and aquariums are so popular with children. The sheer variety of animals present in zoos and the encounters with new creatures excite children and stimulate their imaginations.

The textures, patterns, and colors found in the animal world are a feast for the senses of sight and touch. Animals with fur appeal to children's urge to feel soft, textural things. Colorful feathers, glossy scales, and intriguing patterns are also appealing.

Animals have a variety of unusual smells, too. Scent is another source of unusual, interesting information that children receive from animals. Horses, pet birds, small mammals, and even cats and dogs all have something of a scent signature that may be unique to that species or that animal. One young girl I know frequently buried her nose in her beloved cat's fur, reporting, "She smells like herself . . . aaah."

Children also appreciate the variety of sounds that animals produce. Family pets bark, meow, purr, hiss, growl, and whine. Farm animals cluck, snuffle, moo, snort, stomp, whinny, baa, and bray. Wild birds produce a delightful musical spectrum. "Pocket pets" make soft noises, and pet birds squawk, screech, chatter, and whistle. And when animals in zoos make noises that children can hear, their excitement is palpable—the animal is suddenly that much more real.

Furred, feathered, or scaled animals offer a texture unlike most other things in the classroom. They make unique noises and have unique odors. The multiple, novel sensory qualities of animals that children enjoy have been shown to positively affect children's learning. The love and interest children feel toward animals often fuels children's curiosity and desire to learn.

THE SAME, BUT DIFFERENT

Part of the appeal of animals is that they are so different from us yet also so much like us. They are alive and share our physical needs for food, water, and sleep. They have reactions similar to ours. They may become startled at loud noises and excited at the arrival of a friendly caregiver. They seem to express common human emotions. Animals behave differently depending on the situation, just as we do—they may be shy, tentative, scared, excited, peppy, or tired out. They have distinct personalities, likes and dislikes, even mood swings. In some ways animals are much like children: they are completely dependent on adults for their care and emotional well-being and need to be approached with a different level of sensitivity than that with which one approaches adults.

Animals are also different from humans. We may never understand some animal emotions, communication, and behaviors. Animals offer children a glimpse of their own sometimes mysterious world when they share experiences with children, respond to their overtures, and even enter their world of play.

Gene Myers, a developmental psychologist who studies the relationship between children and animals, explores children's view of animals' same and different qualities in his book *The Significance of Children and Animals*. He states that children see animals as "nonhuman others"; that is, they intuitively recognize that animals are other living creatures based on four key characteristics: agency, affectivity, coherence, and continuity. These four characteristics are universal. All children intuitively recognize them, and each characteristic has a role to play in children's understanding of animals as sentient beings, or "social others." They are essentially the factors that separate a dog from a bookshelf, a toy train, or any other inanimate object that is in a child's life.

First, unlike any toy, animals move and behave of their own accord. They have *agency* and autonomy. Animals do things that are unpredictable and sometimes seem random. They initiate their own behavior. This characteristic offers a child constant novelty. Even a familiar animal, the family dog, for example, is always doing something new and different. By this I don't mean that Fido or Fluffy is spontaneously doing new tricks. I simply mean that she gets up, lies down on the rug, and runs to the window to bark at a squirrel of her own accord. She is relatively autonomous. The dog's agency is one element of her "is-ness" that keeps her so interesting and captivating. An animal may respond to a child's advances (such as a hungry box turtle approaching a strawberry after a child places it in the turtle's food dish), but it is relatively self-directed.

Aside from humans and other animals, no other creatures in a child's life move and act of their own accord. Even robotic or battery-powered pets, which do seem to move and act of their own accord, do not captivate children in the same way live creatures do. Again, this may seem to be common sense, but it's telling. It indicates a genuine awareness that real animals are different than these lifelike toys. And to a young child, the movement and agency an animal demonstrates are very exciting and emotionally powerful.

Animals, Myers says, also "demonstrate what we might call moods, emotions, or ups and downs of energy in response to their world." This is the second quality that Myers describes: animals have affect. Myers explains, "We know that the human mind is especially good at mirroring, or using one's own inner experience to model and try to understand the actions and emotions of another. Children must use this ability to empathize with an animal's *affective* state of being. The child may see the dog is lying down, [resting, and that child senses a] calm, comfortable affect. Perhaps the child will want to interact with the dog and share that state, cuddling up." An animal's affect also signals to children when they should change their behavior. For example, when a child pinches or handles an animal too roughly, the animal may startle or move away from the child. When an excited child squeals and dashes up to a bird in a cage, and that bird startles, jumps off its perch, and flaps wildly against the cage bars, the child may realize that his own behavior had an impact on the bird's state of being. In general, most children use agency and affect as keys to how they will interact with an animal.

Another characteristic that makes animals so powerful to children is coherence. Coherence is a sense of wholeness, especially as it relates to the animal's physical body. The way in which a pet dog moves, any predictability inherent in its actions, what it does in the home, in the yard, and in the dog park are all elements of an animal's coherence: the integration of behavior, physicality, movement, sounds, and other interactions. If the pet dog is injured, ill, or behaves erratically, for example, limping or dragging a hind leg,

it immediately attracts attention and may seem "wrong" in a way that might feel disturbing—a feeling we rarely have if a machine breaks down. We also recognize coherence in our fellow humans, such as in a thirsty coworker rising from the lunch table to get a glass of water; her behavior and movements are part of an organized system that moves with grace and fluidity. If that coworker were a robot and moved with jerky motions and strange cacophonous noises, she would lack the coherence that tells us she's a fellow living creature. Although children may not always understand animals' behavior, it makes intuitive sense.

Myers's fourth quality is continuity. Repeated interactions with an animal can become a relationship. Continuity, in particular, is important because it allows a child to see himself, as a human being, as similar yet still different from the other animal. The interactions between child and animal build on one another and form the basis for a relationship: a connection between that child and that animal. This is very important. Trust may develop as relationships form (as might other feelings, depending on the interactions!). Children may learn to predict an animal's actions and responses, and animals grow more comfortable with children over time and with repeated interactions.

Repeated interactions offer children a chance to simply practice relationship building. Animals do things in response to a child's behavior or actions.

They interact immediately and consistently. Their responses may be negative, positive, or neutral. Children learn what kind of behavior will elicit a positive response, and what behaviors result in inattention or aloofness from the animal. Some behaviors or advances will result in negative feedback (the animal snapping or growling, the animal walking away), which also provides rich material for a child's learning. These repeated interactions allow children to base their behavior on the result of previous interactions: *Last time when I rubbed her chin, she purred; this time she might purr again.* Clearly, repeated interactions with animals are more meaningful than onetime trips to a petting zoo (although those experiences can be special, too! More on that in chapter 5). "The net effect of such repeated interactions," Myers says, "is that the animal can affirm the child's own core sense of self, and help him or her implicitly realize the richness of the human self, which is able in its own ways to connect across species differences with the multi-species world."

COGNITIVE CHALLENGE

Animals are also appealing for the sheer variety of ways children can think about them. Consider how many young children enjoy sorting,

categorizing, and listing things. Some children can recite with zeal lists of species belonging to certain orders or families, such as the young kindergartner I met who knew all the North American frog species' names by heart. Other children love dinosaurs and recall names of dinosaur species, sizes, habitat preferences, and food choices. Many parents and teachers alike are amazed by children's abilities to recall and amass knowledge about certain groups of animals or an exclusive favorite species. There are seemingly unlimited opportunities for children to create categories and group animals. Tell a child with a huge collection of stuffed animals to put all the "sea creatures" together in a basket, and the basket quickly fills with stuffed fish, dolphins, whales, and seals. The challenging and fun cognitive exercise of sorting and categorizing animal varieties encourages many children's love of animals. It also strengthens children's cognitive abilities to sort, order, classify, and group—important and fundamental scientific and mathematical thinking skills.

AFFECTION

One reason children feel so deeply connected to some companion animals is that they share a common language for showing affection. While we use the term *affect* to refer to an animal's mood or emotional state, we use *affection* to refer to fondness or positive feelings for another. Affection in early childhood is associated with a number of physical behaviors, including cuddling, seeking proximity to those we love, making pleasant vocalizations, and touching. These are the same ways that many pets seek and show affection to their owners. When children are asked to describe how their pets show affection toward them, many of them cite these behaviors, as well as tail wagging, purring, jumping up, and following the child. Children and many animals demonstrate affection through touching, holding close, speaking soft words, and cuddling. Thus, when children and animals want to show affection for each other, they have a common language in which to do so.

COMMUNICATION

The unique communication of animals also appeals to children. Animals use a variety of means to communicate, most of it nonverbal. In some cases, whines, barks, purrs, or squawks are messages that children can interpret on their own. Animals don't wait to let others know how they feel. In many cases, animals' communication has little to do with a child's actions, but when it does, that communication is usually immediate and clear. Animals move their bodies in response to the child's advances: A guinea pig may move away, come closer, hide in a corner, or ignore the child altogether. A parakeet may squawk and flutter around its cage, showing fear or excitement or simply reacting to the large hand that suddenly entered her living space. A nervous terrier may growl and snarl if a curious girl comes too close, causing the child to rethink her quick grabs at his ears and alter her behavior to a slow, cautious touch to the dog's shoulder instead. A skin twitch in response to a child's poke may be all it takes to engage a child. That child might seek out a cat's purr by petting her behind the ears, then under the chin, and finally, after the cat nuzzles farther into her hand, on the spot just above her eyes.

Animals' direct messages can also be a welcome contrast to the world of human communication. Young children are constantly at work deciphering and interpreting the subtle rules of human communication, which can contain mixed messages, subtle nuances, or "hidden agendas" below the surface. For example, a child's harried mother may speak sharply and slam the door as she scrambles to pack the children into the car one morning so she can get to work on time. She tells the children she's not angry, yet her face expresses displeasure. The child must then reconcile conflicting messages wondering, *How does she really feel? What does she really think?*

Animals, on the other hand, leave nothing to guesswork. If a dog doesn't like something a child is doing, the dog will snarl, snap, growl, or simply walk away. A bird flies away when a child comes too close. A cat may leave the sofa when a too-noisy child plops down next to her. Hamsters will munch on their food when observed by a still, quiet child, but when disturbed or threatened, they may scurry off to a hiding place in the corner of their cage. These are all direct messages that a child can understand at face value. There is no need for interpretation or teasing apart words, tone of voice, facial expression, and other nonverbal cues to get at the "real" message. This clarity helps children form connections with animals, because their attempts at communication result in clear, unambiguous feedback to which they generally know how to respond. Remember that any response from an animal can be considered a "useful" communication in this regard, because a response in this context means that the animal has received and is responding to the child's attempts at interaction. A positive response from an animal encourages connection by building children's confidence in processing and responding to the communication of another.

IT'S ALL ABOUT ME

Many children respond to an animal's nonverbal or verbal communication with a natural assumption that the animal is speaking or communicating directly with him. This is part of why children respond with such excitement when an animal makes noise. If Noah, a preschooler, greets the classroom bird with a cheerful "Hello!" and the bird squawks in response, it can be very exciting indeed! Or when a dog barks excitedly as a child tosses a ball in the backyard, it can feel to the child as though "the dog is playing with me!" In fact, many animal behaviorists and pet owners alike would argue that indeed the dog is responding to the child with pure excitement and joy, much as a human friend would do.

Many children may speak to household or classroom pets in a quiet whisper, telling it their secrets or troubles of the day. Even adults know that animals are great listeners. They accept without question or judgment the words that we say and the feelings that we share. We can talk to our pets and tell them things we can't tell anyone else. Children know this, too. Children may eagerly search out a household pet at the end of the day, telling the cat how things have gone at a playdate, or what they did at school. Many a curious parent has listened in to these conversations, knowing the child will likely tell the cat more than she'd tell her mom. In the classroom, a child may whisper secret wishes or hopes for the day to a pet turtle, who seems to sit patiently in her tank while the child speaks.

Young children assume that animals can hear and understand them when they are speaking, and often speak to animals in a way similar to the way they speak to babies. The fact that children consistently use this "special speech" to speak to animals indicates a belief that animals relate to language and vocabulary in the same way that children and adults do. Note that children generally do not talk to furniture or inanimate objects, but they do talk to animals. As obvious as this seems, talking to animals illustrates that children assume animals are listening to them, that they understand, and that they will respond to the child's language in some way. Talking to an animal indicates that a child assumes the pet has a desire to communicate with the child.

Consider this simple yet nuanced example: A five-year-old boy, while helping to unload groceries from the car, called to the neighbor's dog, Carter, who appeared to be watching from the yard next door, "We're just unloading the groceries from the car, Cart." This example illustrates that the boy believed that Carter, a Jack Russell terrier, could understand not only the language the boy was using but also the meaning behind the words. (The boy also assumed that the dog was interested in what he was doing based on the fact that the dog appeared to be watching him.) His tone in speaking to the dog was matter-of-fact, the same tone that he would use had it been his sister who was watching.

Clearly, the boy has a sense that Carter shares this world with him and is participating in it in much the same way he is—and was interested in what he was doing. Using the nickname "Cart" instead of the dog's full name also indicates that the boy sees the dog as a peer or a friend, rather than an object or disinterested party. Children rarely have nicknames for inanimate objects. It shows that the boy feels familiarity with Carter, much as one would feel with a human friend.

This example also illustrates that children tend to feel that an animal's behavior is a response to whatever the child is doing (remember that the early childhood years are a very self-centered age). As far as the boy was concerned, if Carter the dog was watching him unload the car, surely it was because he was interested in what the boy was doing and why. Dogs are curious animals, so it's likely that the dog was indeed watching the boy, but it's possible he wasn't. In reality, the dog could have been watching a nearby squirrel, birds in the yard, or something else entirely.

A sense of it being "all about me" is a natural feeling, especially in early childhood. In fact, when asked, most preschoolers in one study indicated that not only did they believe their pets could think and feel, but also that when those pets were thinking, they were thinking *about that child*. When an excited boy is paired with an equally excited dog, it can feel to the child as though the dog knows just what the child is feeling and is responding in kind. This genuine back-and-forth, this sense the child has that the dog knows what he is feeling and that the dog actually shares that feeling is called *attunement*, and it is a feeling that children enjoy in many of their interactions with animals. For example, on Monday morning, Simone tells the classroom goldfish about her busy weekend, and she observes the fish approaching the surface of the water, expecting a few flakes of food. Simone sees the fish's behavior as a direct response to her chatter and presence. This leads her to believe that the fish must be interested in what she is saying. When asked, most children will report that an animal's common everyday behaviors are directed at the child herself, indicating that the child perceives the animal as communicating directly with the child.

VULNERABILITY

In a child's world, adults rule. Adults make most of the decisions. They are the source of love, food, space, shelter, and the other basic elements of survival, pleasure, and comfort. Animals are the only living creatures that children can dominate. Although in our culture we often use the term *dominate* in a somewhat negative tone, I use the word here simply to mean

"to have more power than." This is neither good nor bad, it simply is. When a child is with an animal, she is in charge, if only for a while. When encountering small animals, such as household or classroom pets, children can be the decision makers (how much or when to feed you, whether or not I will pet you, where I will set you down). Even simply feeding an animal at a petting zoo can elicit some of the same feelings of power, and in many cases, it's the earliest memory children have of connecting with animals. Of course, if you ask a child what's special about that experience, he will say things like "the horse came so close I could smell it," or he may describe the light touch of the bird's beak in the palm of his hand. These more subtle qualities of caring can also contribute to the specialness and vulnerability of the moment.

The power of caring for an animal and playing a role in the animal's well-being can be very meaningful for a young child. Especially in their early years, children are busy trying to understand how they are capable and competent. Giving children the opportunity to participate in meaningful caring activities for a vulnerable creature can build tremendous confidence.

FREE SPEECH

Speaking with animals offers children a freedom that is not always felt when speaking to adults. Adults who are concerned with teaching and helping children develop their language skills can seem more focused on the mechanics of what the child is saying than the child's message. Or some well-meaning adults try to help children "talk through" their problems or

offer to help a child process his feelings. For children trying to navigate the already complex world of adult communication, these added pressures can discourage their speaking comfortably and freely.

In contrast, animals listen without question, without demand. They hear what a child has to say and don't press her to say anything more. The family dog doesn't ask a child to elaborate, reason, justify, apologize, or explain. He just listens. This can be very freeing for a child. Children know that they can tell a pet anything and it will be a safe secret. No matter how silly or insignificant a child's feelings may seem, a receptive pet will never laugh, be dismissive, or minimize that child for having those feelings. And isn't this why we adults also talk to animals?

Animals inhabit a world not created by adults, and this affords children a certain freedom as well. Children are free to playact with animals, adapting their behavior and habits. Some very tolerant pets will allow themselves to be involved in children's play, which can be thrilling and gratifying for young children. Young children may become deeply immersed in play involving animals: they may include the family cat as a member of the pretend "camping trip" happening in the living room, or they may have the toy people "visit" the classroom parakeet in her cage. The animal may have a special or "starring role" in the story, and the child feels free to include it.

Of course, adults should closely supervise this play to ensure the safety of both animals and children. The opportunity to express themselves as they wish in front of animals is, for some children, a liberating and valuable quality in the relationship.

EXCITING ABILITIES

Children also find the "magical" qualities of animals in stories and media appealing. Animals often have special powers. They can fly, see in the dark, move with extreme speed, live underwater, scare away monsters—things that children wish they themselves could do. In real life, animals also have special powers: echolocation, acute senses of smell and hearing, the ability to live underwater, climb to the tops of trees, fly, hibernate, freeze, burrow underground, jump high, breathe underwater, walk on walls, hang upside down, and more! These exciting abilities make animals appealing and instantly captivating for children. Because they have special abilities, these animals hold children's attention and can be great teachers.

Children's love for animals and their many abilities can be expressed through pretend play. When children can play at being animals, they're free of the limitations of being human! They imagine that they can climb the tallest trees and swing from vines and branches. They can fly in the clouds, swim in the deepest oceans, or strike fear into the hearts of weaker, smaller creatures. Playing with these fantasies is not only fun, but it can help children feel powerful and strong, too. As discussed in chapter 3, it also helps children build empathy and compassion toward animals and other people and deepens their positive feelings for them.

PROCESSING FEELINGS

For many children, animals, especially pets in the home, represent safety and security. They are familiar, they are safe to talk to, and they are a source of comfort and love. Because animals are appealing and reassuring, they are often a source of comfort that children will seek out to process their feelings. When my own children reacted with fear to a loud thunderstorm, it was comforting to them to see that the dog was also afraid. As our dog Nina paced around the bedroom and whined, the children spoke in soothing tones to her and petted her lovingly, even sharing their beloved blankies with her. Offering comfort to her seemed to help them find the inner resources needed to find comfort for themselves as well. The next time there was a thunderstorm, the children's concern for Nina overshadowed their own fears about the thunder. They set to work trying to keep the dog comfortable and seemed to forget their own past fears.

In a classroom, educators can support children when they see them feeling nervous or anxious. If you have pets in the classroom, encourage children to think about how those pets are feeling, for example, during a storm or a fire drill. Even if the classroom gerbils seem indifferent or unaware, it can help the children to consider the experience from the perspective of these small animals. If the children are feeling nervous about the fire drill, for example, they may project those feelings onto the gerbils. If they don't project their feelings onto the gerbils, it is still fodder for a good conversation. You might ask, "Why aren't the gerbils afraid? How do they know they are safe? How do we know we are safe? The same way, or different?" The children will have many ideas for how to comfort or reassure the gerbils. Then, later, when the children are feeling nervous themselves, you can remind them that they already have many good ideas about how to calm nervous feelings: "Remember how we helped the gerbils when they were afraid? We spoke in quiet voices, and we stayed close by. Let's try that with each other." There are many opportunities, then, for children to work through their fears and anxieties by projecting their own feelings onto animals, then giving the animals the care and tenderness that they themselves desire.

Though they might not be able to explain it, children love animals for plenty of reasons. Animals can offer novel, multisensory experiences that are stimulating and powerful. They respond to children in ways that are familiar and easy to understand, yet also exciting and delightful. On a more subtle level, animals allow children a safe sounding board with whom they can practice speaking, sorting out their feelings, and being caregivers. Animal characters, stuffed animals, and toys serve as tools for children to explore feelings, direct their own life circumstances, and resolve their own struggles. And animals sometimes comfort children in a way nobody else can.

Midway through the school year, Lateesha enters a preschool classroom for the first time. She has just moved here, and she feels shy and nervous about her new school and all the children she doesn't know. When she enters the room, a small group of children crowds around her, excited to show her their favorite thing about school: the class-room pet, a box turtle. They talk over each other, excited to share their knowledge about the turtle:

Mohammed: This is the turtle, her name is Sandy! She eats worms and strawberries. We read her stories sometimes.

Daniel: Sometimes we give her dandelion leaves, too.

Ali: And crickets! Sandy loves crickets!

Daniel: Yeah, but you have to help her find the crickets!

Mohammed: She doesn't see very well, so we help her find the crickets.

Ali: She has that light, on the top of her tank. That light helps her see. That light gives her vitamins. That's her soaking dish there. She likes to soak and take baths in that soaking dish. You can't put toys in her tank.

Daniel: Sometimes she poops in the soaking dish!

Holly: She's scared of loud noises. She doesn't like when you tap on her tank. She likes to go outside. Sometimes we take her outside to the grass.

Daniel: She stretches her head way out when we take her outside! She loves it outside!

Ali: And she hides under that box when she's tired and wants to get away. It's her quiet place.

Holly: And you can only touch her if Miss West says so. And you have to wash your hands with soap.

As Lateesha's curiosity is piqued, it overrides some of her apprehension. The other children share in the role of welcoming her by telling her all about the turtle: its name, how they care for it, and what she can expect the turtle to do from time to time. They share with Lateesha their cognitive understanding of the turtle (what it eats, why it has a soaking dish, what the light is for). In doing so, they indicate their awareness of the turtle's unique physical needs, its vulnerability, and their caring roles (by mentioning Sandy's need for food, how they help her find crickets, the fact that she cannot see well, the fact that she "doesn't like when you tap on the tank"). When they talk about the turtle stretching its head out while outdoors, the children demonstrate their shared sense that the turtle has feelings—the turtle's behavior is evidence that the turtle is happy outside. They have demonstrated the development of their scientific thinking skills when they described their observations about the turtle's behavior and the conclusions they've made about what that behavior means. Finally, the turtle is an opportunity for the children to connect with Lateesha, as they tell her everything that their classroom community does with the turtle. In a seemingly simple interaction around a beloved animal, much more is happening than meets the eye.

Animals invite children into the fantastical world of other living creatures. The way animals break down social barriers can help quell nervous feelings in children or can give focus to an overstimulated group. When a new child enters the class, the children may enjoy sharing stories about their favorite animal or playing animal games or charades. Children and adults alike often open up when given the opportunity to talk about animals and their feelings about animals. And adults can remember how it feels to explore the mysterious animal world for the first time and allow children to experience it for themselves.

How Animal Interactions Support Children's Development

A young baby follows a furry pet cat with her eyes as it trots through the living room. She stretches out her fingertips to touch its soft fur as it passes. The cat is one of the first things the baby reaches for in her young life.

Preschoolers react with palpable excitement when a puppy is brought into the classroom for show and tell. And they quickly learn from the puppy's responses that they may not pull its tail or grab its ears!

Toddlers giggle and even tremble with excitement upon the cautious approach of a family of ducklings during a field trip to a local park. The excitement they feel inspires them to talk to each other and their teacher, trying out some new words such as *duckling*, *pond*, and *paddle*.

In this chapter we explore how children's relationships with animals influence their development. What is happening when children engage the animal world? How do interactions with animals affect children's values and self-identity? What can we learn about children's development by watching their interactions with animals? Why is it important for adults to pay attention to the shared world of children and animals? Much of today's child development literature addresses children's relationships with other people—children, siblings, parents, caregivers, and extended family. Recent child development research has demonstrated the impact of children's early relationships on their sense of well-being, overall physical health, and other factors.

However, there is also a growing body of research that examines the relationships between children and animals. Children's interactions with animals are different from pushing a button on an automated toy, playing an instrument, or even interacting with other children and adults. Early

interactions with animals can be crucial experiences in young children's development of many values and models for caring. Among other things, animals can help children develop a sense of "self" and "other," explore a healthy two-way relationship, and build ethical values. Although there is a great deal we are only beginning to understand, a number of studies have found that the way children relate to animals is unique and significant and has a lifelong influence. This chapter examines some of what we know about that influential relationship.

LEARNING HOW TO CARE

Engaging with animals allows children to tune in, for however long or short a time, to a world outside themselves. Even before caring for real animals, children play at taking care of stuffed animals based on what they see adults doing with babies or pets. They demonstrate the behavior and the attitudes that they've seen modeled by adults. They relish the opportunity to care for live animals such as household or classroom pets. And since in many cultures much of the caregiving and nurturing is done by females, children demonstrate an awareness of traditional gender roles as they practice giving care. In some cases, animals can help children overcome traditional gender roles about caregiving. Certainly caring for animals is not the only way that children relate to animals, but it has important implications for children's developing view of animals.

Caring and Stuffed Animals

Because so many babies are given plush toys at a young age, children's associations with animals, even toy ones, start early. Some children cuddle with stuffed animals from an early age and often treasure that first teddy bear or stuffed dog on into college. Many people wonder if a child's strong bond to a stuffed animal is as "valuable" or important as a child's bond to a live animal such as a pet. The relationship between children and stuffed animals is, of course, different from the relationship that a child has with a real animal, but stuffed animals offer several opportunities for learning. Beyond their cute and cuddly qualities, stuffed animals can aid children's development by growing a child's understanding of the "self" and "other" and by providing a bridge to the world of real animal relationships.

When a baby treasures and loves a stuffed animal, he may be attaching to the toy for a variety of reasons. Infants and toddlers often become attached to objects such as stuffed toys, dolls, blankets, or pacifiers. These objects are known as *transitional objects*, a term coined by the researcher Donald Woods Winnicott in 1953. As a transitional object, a plush toy helps a child transition to a new way of thinking about the world. Sometimes people interpret the "transition" in the phrase *transitional object* to mean a time of transition, during which these objects certainly may provide comfort and security. In fact, Winnicott's phrase actually refers to that time in a baby's life when he is transitioning from a psychological place of feeling "one with everything" to the sense that he is a separate, dependent being. Stuffed animals often serve as representations of a baby's connection to the "not me" world outside herself. They become very important to infants around the time that they are first differentiating themselves from their mothers and realizing they are a part of, but not one with, a larger system.

This major developmental stage is known as individuation in infancy. All infants experience it, regardless of race, gender, health, or background. Attachment to an object during this stage provides a child with a sense of security or a psychological link to his mother. When an object is used again and again (for example, when a parent hands a crying baby his blankie), it becomes an object of extremely high value to that baby. It is a source of comfort, security, and positive feelings. Childhood attachment to specific comfort objects, such as teddy bears and stuffed puppies, is part of a child's development of his sense of self and also can contribute to his sense of caring for others.

I must stress here that while children may become attached to an object that is a replica of an animal, I don't generally interpret that as attaching to *that particular species* of animal. In actuality, the infant may be attaching to a number of things. She may be attaching to the smell of the toy, the feel of the fabric, or even the positive memory of receiving the gift. She may smell her mother on the stuffed cat, and this brings her comfort. Perhaps this stuffed kitty is the first "not me" object that the child has ever owned. Perhaps that stuffed kitty provides other psychological anchors, such as a memory of the arrival of a baby brother or a special time with Grandma. While a child may not be attached to a specific animal at this stage, stuffed animals can help children develop past a sense of "not me" to advanced roles in caring for animals.

For the child who is beginning to love animals and feel a sense of curiosity about them, cuddly stuffed animals can be a good way to indulge and expand this interest. A cat-loving child receives plush kitties and cats as gifts, which actually may help to later deepen her interest in the animal species itself. If she continues to express interest in cats, intentional parents, caregivers, and family friends may nurture her curiosity by supporting her experience through books, games, toys, and experiences with real cats.

This is one way that a parent can bridge the gap between a child's attachment to a representation of an animal and an attachment to *an actual animal.* In other words, nurturing that child's strong feelings toward a plush animal, while initially an attachment to something else (such as the scent of mother, a memory, or another positive association), may serve to help strengthen her initial curiosity on a long road of learning and discovery. Strengthening a child's curiosity may lead to a love for that species of animal simply because it reinforces that child's good feelings about animals, especially in children who tend to develop a strong affinity for animals in general. And good feelings about animals lead to more good feelings about animals. Research shows that the more positive early experiences a child has with animals in their many contexts, the more likely that child will grow up to be an animal lover.

Care Begets Care

Care is a significant part of animal relationships that can build on children's early experiences with stuffed animal and live animal interactions. Caring is a two-way relationship. The experience of caring for another creature increases children's awareness of others. As children develop their cognitive and physical abilities, they are able to practice caring for other living creatures. While children will not directly care for most animal species, they can develop a wider understanding of themselves and the world of animals by participating in a care relationship with a few animals.

Providing young children not just with opportunities to see and be near animals, but giving them the chance to actually be involved in caring for animals is vitally important. Research shows that even very young children have a solid grasp of what animals need to survive and thrive. This finding is important because it tells us that young children have an innate sense of connection to animals as other living beings with needs. Research has also shown that children who are involved in caring for animals later develop affinity for the natural world and other animals, thus demonstrating the power of early opportunities to connect with animals. Early experiences of caring for animals can grow into feelings of stewardship toward the natural world. When children participate in the day-to-day routines of caring for animals, such as feeding, watering, grooming, or cleaning a tank, they develop a sense of what "caring" actually means, what it means to "give care," and that there are many different forms that caring may take. Even when children only interact with an animal once, such as at a petting zoo, but have a chance to care for it through feeding or grooming, there is a positive impact on the child. When children care for animals and receive a positive response from the animal, it also strengthens their confidence in themselves as creatures able to give care.

As children practice caring for animals, they learn social and cognitive skills that increase their connection and caring to the world outside themselves. In the book *Children and Nature*, scholars Gene Myers and Carol Saunders identify three elements of caregiving that all caregivers experience.

The first element of caregiving is simply *being aware of another's need*. For children to be aware of an animal's needs, they must pay close attention to the animal. They need to be aware of its behavior and what the pet communicates. While human infants cry out when they need to be fed, animals are not always so obvious in their communication. So how can a child know that an animal has needs? After spending time with the animal and making observations about when it eats, what it eats, and more, the child begins to know that animal. Even a child who is just encountering an animal for the first time may notice subtle body language or other cues that let her know the animal has needs. A guinea pig scoots up close to a food dish, for example, or a bird turns away when overstimulated.

The act of caring also requires that an individual *put another's needs first*. The child will put the needs of the animals above his or her own when the child takes action to care for the animal. Many parents or educators have witnessed this. For example, a child who is busy playing with his toys might notice that his pet dog is standing at the door, doing an "I need to go out" dance. The child must put his own desires (to continue playing) aside for a short time and get up to let the dog out or go find his parent or caregiver to call attention to the dog's needs. Or consider the girl who upon entering kindergarten each morning runs to feed the classroom bird before even hanging up her coat and backpack.

The third element of caring is *acknowledgment by the recipient of care*. This doesn't mean that an animal will send a thank-you card, cuddle, or even nuzzle a child's hand in response. It simply means that the animal will respond in some way. The child may see an animal eat the food it's been given or watch a bird hop around in the yard in search of seeds, and she knows that animal is behaving this way "because I provided that food." She is witnessing the animal's direct response to being cared for. In one preschool, children were taking turns brushing a goat. The simple act of standing still, allowing the children to brush him, was the goat's way of responding to the children's act of caring. The goat could have moved away, stepped restlessly with its feet, or even tried to butt at the children. All of these movements would have been responses for the children to interpret. It's important to give children the opportunity to watch animals and spend time with them in order to see the reactions and behavior of animals in response to their care attempts. An animal's reaction can reinforce or redirect the children's behavior toward the animal and can inform children about their ability to trust their instincts when caring for others.

Children can use their caring abilities in many ways. They can feed, pet, or groom animals, clean their cages or tanks, create things for them (such as nesting boxes, toys, or climbing structures), and talk or sing to them. Chapters 5 and 6 provide more ways that educators and parents can offer children opportunities to give genuine care to animals. The important thing is that children develop their awareness of and response to another's needs by feeding, grooming, and doing other day-to-day chores related to animal caregiving. When a child is participating in the care and feeding of a hamster so that it stays healthy and happy, she is also doing important work for her own development and growth, too.

Gender Roles and the Care Relationship

The care relationship with animals can be especially valuable for boys. Researchers have found support that boys are socially conditioned against being caregivers at a very young age. Animals provide boys with the opportunity to care for and nurture something.

In many early childhood classrooms, young children of both genders engage in dramatic play, practicing "housekeeping" and learning to dress, diaper, cuddle, rock, and feed dolls. As they grow older, boys tend to lose interest in playing house or engaging in caregiving play with dolls, if they

ever developed an interest in these activities at all. Many early childhood educators and parents have observed that after about age three (although it varies from child to child), boys and girls naturally seek out same-sex friendships, and boys' group play behavior tends toward rough-and-tumble, aggressive play or play with blocks and vehicles. On the other hand, all-girl groups tend to gravitate toward domestic play, dramatic play, and play involving caregiving and nurturing. While these behavior differences are natural and common, some educators find them disconcerting. But they're not inherently bad; it's just the way gender-based groups tend to behave. Adults may encourage children to engage in less gender-stereotyped behavior, but these play choices are also natural and normal for young children.

However, animals are a great equalizer. In a study at Purdue University, Gail F. Melson and her colleagues conducted research on the amount of time children spent caring for babies and pets. They found that by the time children are about eight years old, girls are more involved in baby care than are boys, while both boys and girls care for pets in the home about equally. Significantly, animal care remains a relatively gender-neutral form of care-giving in which many boys engage freely. Perhaps a five-year-old boy who shows no interest in dolls or "parenting" will be content to care for, groom, and nurture a toy dog, or he may be deeply engaged in caring for the class-room lizard. Since most young boys see females in the primary role of caregiver, toy animals—or better yet, live animals—offer young boys a great opportunity to practice caring for other living things.

In addition to holding boys' interest longer, live animal care and animal toys also offer a "safe" place for boys to develop and practice their nurturance skills with no fear of bias, judgment, or other social ramifications. In another study, Melson and her re-search team examined the attitudes of four-year-old and seven-year-old children. They wanted to under-stand young children's attitudes about caring roles. Researchers showed the children line drawings of male and female children, teenagers, young adults, and older adults and then asked the children to select the picture of an appropriate caregiver for different subjects. For example, when asked, "Who could take care of a baby?" the children selected images of adult females, whom the children labeled "mom-mies," as best able to provide care for babies. Similarly, children of both ages selected images of adult or teenage females as appropriate caregivers for human infants, young children, and the elderly. However, when asked, "Who could take care of a dog or cat?" the children selected images of both males and females.

It's not within the scope of this book to comprehensively evaluate boys' and girls' gender-based play behavior, but along with a decline in boys' dra-matic play behaviors comes a set of cultural expectations placed on many children. During this stage, boys and girls are exploring their own sex dif-ferences, demonstrating a preference for same-sex playmates, and trying to make sense of what makes something a "girl toy" and a "boy toy." Earnest girls

and boys may discourage some boys from playing house or playing with dolls, firmly reminding them that dolls are "girl toys." Similarly, the targeted toys that adults provide for girls and boys can continue to maintain children's ideas of caregiving roles. Toys traditionally associated with caregiving and housekeeping are purchased more often for girls and are more likely to be used by girls.

Melson points out that during the age when boys move away from caregiving roles in their play is a good time to engage them in play situations and opportunities where they are free to be caregivers in a nonthreatening and gender-neutral context. Caring for classroom pets and household animals gives boys opportunities to openly express affection and love in their interactions with other creatures. One study also found that competence in cooperation, social-emotional understanding, and social play behavior (such as dramatic play) improves among boys who have pets or have access to pets. Boys who interact regularly with pets respond better to nonverbal cues, are more socially literate, and cooperate better with others.

EXPLORING THE CARE RELATIONSHIP

Relationships with animals create a space for children to explore and develop interpersonal skills that will influence other areas of their lives. Caring for animals helps children explore their own power, strengthens their skills of observing and interpreting, and offers children a number of physiological benefits.

Power and Vulnerability

Why are experiences with animals unique for children? Why is brushing a goat different than say, offering a cookie to a playmate or sharing a toy? The playmate will certainly appreciate the cookie or a toy. What makes some animal interactions unique is that animals are vulnerable and dependent on children. These experiences can build confidence in young children because, again, they require the child to be receptive to the animal's communication—is the animal responding favorably to being brushed? If so, the child may do it again or try other actions to get another favorable response. When the child sees that he has been successful, it can boost his confidence. He realizes that he's capable of reading and responding to cues. He has done something to help another creature. He sees that he can use his power over this vulnerable creature in a positive way.

Even very young children may react with alarm or panic when an animal is harmed or on the verge of being harmed. Many a young child has been known to burst into tears at the sight of a dead squirrel at the side of the road, or to be saddened or righteously indignant when a classmate kills a ladybug. Many children's innate sense of the value of an animal leads to recognizing an animal's vulnerability and can develop into a strong sense of justice and peacekeeping. This sense of justice arises from the child's own feelings that

the animal has inherent worth, not necessarily from the judgment of "right" and "wrong" that adults apply to situations and behaviors. As Stephen Kellert notes, with exposure children become "cognizant of the autonomous rights of other life and begin to develop feelings of responsibility for care and considerate treatment of nature independent of being punished by adults for improper behavior."

Some adults are justly concerned about children who are aggressive in exploring animals' vulnerabilities. While there will always be those children who relish the opportunity to stomp on ants or pull the wings off butterflies, I contend that these behaviors don't necessarily indicate psychopathic tendencies, as so many parents and even some educators seem to fear. Rather, these are simple ways that children play with their own power, experimenting with their own capabilities and strengths. Often an act like stomping on an insect may not even register in a child's mind as a harmful act. In some cases, when a child does this, say, while on a walk with his classmates, the alarmed and upset reaction it provokes in other children can cause a child to feel powerful and strong, an attractive feeling indeed! The adults involved in such a situation should remember that strong reactions to the behavior might serve to reinforce that experimental behavior. Occasionally the experiment can surprise a child. Many children will impulsively squash a ladybug without realizing it will kill the ladybug, then react with surprise, guilt, or shame when they realize what they've done. Of course, I am not implying that those behaviors should be encouraged, but teachers and parents should remember that these situations are part of how children learn about animals and can intentionally guide them toward more gentleness. As children age, these sorts of interactions with animals tend to decrease and eventually taper off completely. As most adults know, modeling positive behavior can be a powerful lesson for young children. Treating insects and other animals with kindness and gentleness is one way to discourage destructive experimentation. Chapter 5 describes "humane education," which is one approach for creatively dealing with this behavior. Obviously, if the child is causing harm to or scaring an animal, it's best for the adult to intervene.

If you ever see a child consistently going out of her way to kill insects, taking great delight in it, trying to injure other animals, or playacting or talking frequently about injuring animals, you should watch the child closely for other behaviors that might suggest deeper psychological issues, and consult with a children's mental health professional or school psychologist if you have concerns.

Observing Cause and Effect

As children experiment with their own power in animal interactions, they develop their observational skills and a sense of cause and effect. A poke or pinch may just be the child trying to get the animal to respond. This kind of interaction is a basic "scientific method" for learning about the world of animals. Children ask themselves questions: How can I make the creature do something? Will it respond to me? What power do I have here? Does it like/not like this touch? Can it see me/feel me? They can answer their questions by observing the animal's response. Through observing cause-and-effect interactions, children learn about the animal's world. More importantly, by exploring cause and effect, children develop the skills to continue to learn about the world through observation, theorizing, trial and error, and applying their knowledge. The more opportunities children have to approach or attempt to interact with an animal, the more responses they get, and the wider becomes their repertoire of behavior and information about that behavior.

I once brought a box turtle into a kindergarten classroom, and the children squealed with delight when the turtle made her way across the carpet toward them. Their animated behavior and the noise of their "whispering"

escalated with their excitement, and within a few seconds, the turtle stopped moving. At this point the children "shh-ed" each other and reminded one another to "be still, or the turtle won't come over here." Based on their observations of the turtle's response, they quickly learned they needed to settle down and be calm. The children—even children who had never before seen a live turtle—interpreted the turtle's response to their noise and wiggling (not moving, retreating into its shell) to mean the turtle wasn't comfortable. Sure enough, when they settled down and stopped talking, the turtle crept forward once again. The children expressed a shared desire to protect the turtle's well-being and offer it a safe environment. They showed remarkable self-control and self-regulation when trying to alter the group's behavior to better suit their shared perception of what the turtle needed. They wanted it to explore, to move. They didn't need to be told how to create those conditions. They figured it out quickly together without the help of an adult. This short amount of time carefully watching the turtle's behavior provided the children with opportunities to practice their observation skills. They practiced the skills of self-regulation, cooperation, and collaboration when they decided together (and coached one another) on quieting their bodies and voices to better react to the turtle.

Adults also have a significant role in the way they frame children's observations and interactions. The way adults speak to children about their advances toward animals has a powerful impact on a child's sense of competence and view of animal relationships. In reaching out and touching animals, young children are learning to make the distinctions between, for example, how to grab a hefty toy truck and how to touch a small fuzzy gerbil. As mentioned earlier, a child's intentions are usually good despite a tendency to grab or pet an animal roughly.

Instead of assuming the worst and responding sharply, adults can support young children in sorting out their physicality by making statements like the following: "When you tugged on the gerbil's tail, she tried to get away. I think she was hurt or scared. What do you think?" and "Brownie didn't seem to like that when you tried to put her in a box. What did she do?" First, these statements help the child observe, articulate, and identify the animal's response—especially responses of discomfort or dislike—to his actions. Second, the child is asked to reflect on what happened and practice interpreting how the animal expressed its dislike. The statements aren't shaming and don't imply that the child's intentions were bad, but they still help the child review and correct behaviors. In another situation, a parent

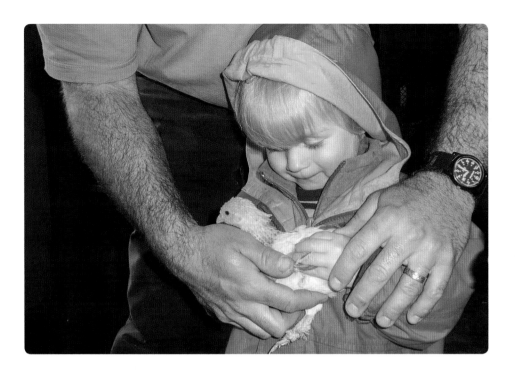

could point out the ways an animal expresses approval for the child's actions. "The dog is wagging her tail when you pet her gently like that! Do you think she likes it?" and "That cat is purring so loudly when you scratch her chin. She must enjoy that so much. You know just how to make her feel good." Here, the parent is validating the child's actions and helping him to see the positive cues the animal is offering.

All adults learned to touch and respond to animals through these same kinds of repeated and varying interactions with animals, and children are beginning that same journey of learning. To help children develop ways to learn about animals, adults can model careful observation, gentleness, and sensitivity toward animals. Adults can show children how to hold animals, supporting their bodies and petting them gently. For many children, holding an animal, whether a chicken or a gerbil or a goat or a guinea pig, can be an exciting experience. A sudden movement by the animal can startle and perhaps even frighten a child. This may lead the child to drop the animal or make a loud noise. Again, remember, when this happens, the child isn't trying to be rough or to hurt the animal. The experience of holding an animal is a new one and one that takes practice in order to feel calm and to know what to expect. Adults can support children's learning by patiently showing them how to safely hold animals, staying close to a child who's holding

an animal, encouraging the child in how and where she is supporting the animal, and talking with the child as she holds the animal.

"See how the gerbil runs up your arm? Does that tickle? Try to hold still if you can. She uses her tail to help her balance." This sort of narration can help a child understand what the animal is doing and why. It also lets the child know that the animal's behavior is normal and natural (because the adult's voice doesn't sound surprised or scared). Telling the child what the animal is doing and how she's moving just helps her get used to the movements of an animal.

These things seem obvious to an adult, but to a young child who's just learning how to handle different animals, these experiences are very important. They help her understand what's happening and predict what's going to happen. They also help her to sort out the wide range of differences in how different animals move. Gerbils move differently than birds, goats, and dogs. There are lots of movements and behaviors that a child who's just getting to know animals is trying to sort, identify, and understand. Learning to observe and then act upon observations is a huge developmental step for a child.

Clear Communication Leads to More Clear Communication

Animals also offer children a number of ways to develop and "test" their social skills through care and observation. As adults, we often strive to make our responses and affirmations of a child's advances very clear, so that the child will know she's appreciated, will feel good about doing something positive, and will want to repeat the behavior in the future. We say "thank you" and "I appreciate that" and "you were very helpful at cleanup time!"

In the case of animals, however, more covert communication requires the child to interpret the behavior by reading nonverbal cues. The child is forced to be aware of sometimes subtle changes in animal behavior to determine whether his advances have been well received. If the animal likes it, the animal will respond favorably to the child. If not, the child receives immediate feedback and occasionally even a chance to "repair" the interaction or try again with a change in behavior. The goal is to elicit a positive response from the animal, and most children will try repeatedly to make positive connections with animals through physical interaction. They want the kitty to purr or the dog to wag its tail.

When Sadie, the class rabbit, responds to a child's tentative offer of a carrot by stretching up her head and nibbling on the carrot, the child receives a message: "What you are doing gives Sadie pleasure, and it helps Sadie." This is what I mean when I refer to feedback from the animal. Even behavior such as hiding, shrinking away, or ignoring an advance altogether tells the child something about Sadie. And the child can interpret Sadie's response many different ways: perhaps "you're moving too quickly," or "you're making too much noise," or possibly even "some rabbits don't like carrots." Frequent and repeated interactions with the animal will help the child make subtle distinctions about the rabbit's behavior in response to his advances. As a child adapts his behavior to respond to the animal, he gains confidence in his own ability to relate to another being. The feedback he receives makes an impact on his own self-worth and trust in his ability to "read" communication from another species.

But what if children are unable to interact directly with an animal? Can the interaction still be significant? Even a goldfish can offer children opportunities to refine their communication skills. When Alvarez runs to the fish tank and slaps the glass, the fish scatter in a cloud of bubbles, disappearing into a ceramic "cave" in their tank. Alvarez can tell immediately that the fish were startled, and he wants them to come back out and swim around normally. He stands still, keeping his hands at his sides, and waits for them to come out. He may even whisper to them. When they do return, he resists the urge to put his hands on the tank, and just keeps his body still, a response to his learning that the fish "didn't like it" when he slapped the glass. He has figured out how to respond through clear communication.

Or consider the complex act of feeding an animal. To interact in this way, a child has to engage some pretty sophisticated skills of interpreting and responding to the animal's cues. She must first determine *how* to offer the food, based on what she's seen others do or what she knows about the animal. Does she offer it to the pet from her open palm? Put it in a dish? Set it on the floor of an animal's cage and stand back? Repeated interactions, either those she's witnessed others having or interactions she herself has shared with an animal, teach a child how to behave when she wants a specific outcome or response from a pet.

Nadira wants to offer an earthworm to a box turtle, a classroom pet. She's had lots of practice and opportunities to observe the turtle's response to her movements. She approaches the turtle's tank quietly and calmly, as she's seen adults do in the past, and as she herself has done. She's learned through trial and error just how slowly and quietly to move. If she moves quickly, she knows the turtle will withdraw into its shell, ending the back-and-forth between the two. Nadira gently places the worm on the turtle's feeding dish and then removes her hand from the tank. She quietly stands by, while the turtle gobbles up the worm. Nadira is all smiles. The turtle's response to her overtures was direct feedback that she was "doing it right." She got the result she wanted (the turtle ate the worm) because she was responsive to the turtle's actions and she was sensitive to her own movements and how the turtle would perceive them. This type of engaging interaction can be powerful for young children. Interacting directly with an animal is exciting, and as we know, seeing a pet eat food that has been offered is satisfying. This acknowledgment is very important for a child when engaging with animals and can be the validation that her efforts are worthwhile and needed.

Children develop communication skills as they experiment with different actions, trying out different behaviors and observing as animals respond in kind. *What happens if I do this? What will the animal do if I pet it this way?* Animals' direct messages can help build children's confidence in their ability to interpret and respond favorably (or unfavorably) to creatures in their care, which continues a cycle of further care and response. A dog paces and whines near the door, and it's pretty clear what the dog wants: to go outside. These unambiguous communications that animals present are refreshing for young children, who are constantly having to sort out the meaning behind adults' messages.

Children are always learning more than one thing at a time. The following story demonstrates how children can learn and practice several developmental skills during a relatively short animal interaction.

Even the smallest of animals warrants care and consideration. At a late-spring preschool picnic, a class of twenty-seven children and their teachers and parents are gathered in a large outdoor park with numerous oak trees. To the delight of the children, there are dozens of fuzzy, black-striped caterpillars on the tree trunks and the ground.

An older girl, Ranjana, is showing a younger boy, Oliver, how to carefully pick up a caterpillar, so as not to injure it or harm one of its many hairlike legs. She had been picking up caterpillars for much of the morning, carrying them around and returning them to the same spot where she got them.

Ranjana (*watching Oliver as he tries to remove a caterpillar from the tree trunk*): Be careful so you don't hurt its legs. It likes to cling like that to the tree bark. You have to let it climb onto your finger first. Don't pull it or its legs will come off.

Oliver extends a flattened hand just above where the caterpillar is, and the caterpillar eventually inches onto his hand.

Ranjana: Now just hold your hand still. Move real slowly. They can hold on good with their legs, but they can still fall. Don't let him fall.

After a minute or so, Oliver decides he no longer wants to hold the caterpillar, and Ranjana helps him put it back on the tree.

Ranjana: Put him back where you got him. He has to go back on the tree where you got him. He needs to be there. Right where you got him.

The caterpillar doesn't leave the boy's hand when he lays it against the tree trunk. He pulls it off his hand with his thumb and fingers.

> Ranjana: Don't squeeze him too hard! You'll squeeze him too hard! Don't squeeze and kill him!
>
> *Oliver carefully puts the (non-squished) caterpillar back on the tree where Ranjana is pointing (very close to the exact spot where he picked up the caterpillar), and it clings to the tree bark, continuing its journey up the tree.*

This exchange illustrates a number of points. First, notice how much knowledge Ranjana had about how to move in order to get the caterpillar. She had spent time collecting caterpillars that morning, so she had lots of practice lifting them off the tree bark and holding them. To get this knowledge, she had to have tried several different techniques of lifting the caterpillar from the tree bark, and she had to have been paying attention to subtle differences in the caterpillars' responses to notice (and then generalize) that the caterpillars "hold on good with their legs." She realizes that the legs are fragile and that the way to ensure the caterpillar doesn't get injured is for Oliver to let it climb onto his hand, instead of potentially pulling too hard and injuring the caterpillar.

Notice also how important it was to Ranjana that Oliver pick up and hold the caterpillar properly, so it wouldn't fall or get squeezed too hard. It is very important to her that the caterpillar should be kept safe, simply because it is a living thing and that matters. Clearly it is important to Oliver also, as he follows her directions to keep the caterpillar safe and does his best to be gentle with it.

Finally, notice that Ranjana was very concerned that the caterpillar go back exactly where it had been picked up. Maybe she recognized that the caterpillar was on its way up to the leaves of the tree (for a bite to eat). Maybe she assumed the caterpillar had traveled a long way up the trunk of the tree. Regardless, it was very important to her that Oliver place it back on the tree where it had been before. In her mind, the caterpillar needed to be put back exactly where it had been picked up. This simple encounter demonstrates several developmental milestones. Ranjana showed sensitivity to the size and vulnerability of the animal and worked to make her friend Oliver aware of it, too. Her sense that the caterpillars needed to go back to their original places on the trees shows an awareness that the animals have agency—they had their own plans for the day, apparently going up the trees. Ranjana was serving as the teacher with Oliver when she instructed him how to pick up and hold the caterpillars. Both children used self-control, and demonstrated self-regulation in holding the caterpillars "just so" and by putting them back on the trees. By placing them on the trees instead of simply tossing them to the ground, the children were considering the caterpillars' needs (or their perception of the caterpillars' needs), which also demonstrates empathy. The children's demonstration of care and compassion during the entire interaction also reinforces the idea that children respond to animals because they value animals intrinsically.

Attachment and Secure Relationships

Attachment theory addresses the relational dynamics all people experience based on their earliest relationships, often with a parent or other caregiver. Simply put, a child's early relationships set the stage for how that child will approach most future relationships. These early relationships may be with parents, siblings, caregivers, or extended family. But what about pets? What effect do early relationships with animals have on children's development of future relationships with animals? Several research studies have found that children's early bonds with animals influence their models and frameworks for their lifelong relationships with animals.

Recent research has looked at how pets can help children feel emotionally secure. One study looked at young children's attitudes toward their pets and found evidence of relational attachment. For example, a child believes that her mother loves her. She believes that her father loves her. And, it turns out, almost all children surveyed believe that their pets "love them very much," demonstrating a level of attachment to animals. Another interesting finding is that the children in this study believed that their pets knew when they were sick, sad, or otherwise in need of some attention. This, too, supports the notion of strong attachment bonds between children and animals. The relationship has the quality of *attunement*, in which a child feels that she understands the animal and the animal understands her. A strong attachment to a pet does not in any way substitute for the attachment that a child has for a primary parent or caregiver, and the two relationships are not of the same caliber. But the strong bonds children feel toward their animals can add to the children's feelings of security and acceptance. Children feel more confident and have improved self-esteem when they have reasonably secure attachments in their world. Attachment and attunement can begin to build on each other. When a child experiences that attunement, she is practicing perspective taking. Any time a child looks at the world through the eyes of an animal, she gets practice in empathy, which can lead to more feelings of attachment.

We know that children can form very strong attachments to their pets, be they pets in the home or classroom. Not only do those attachments help develop empathy and security, they offer children other benefits as well. What may seem to the casual observer to be a simple encounter between a child and an animal is actually something much bigger. The child is building his sense of self, and he is incorporating feedback that he gets from the dog as he learns about his own value. For example, the time a child spends reading to a dog is special, because the dog is paying attention to him and responding to the tone in his voice. The boy and the dog are experiencing attunement, a shared sense of safety and security. A young girl may appear to be absentmindedly stroking her cat, but those moments she spends with the cat are powerful, and the girl may be experiencing deep peace and contentment, relaxing together with her cat. Her breathing is relaxed, her heart rate slows, and she feels safe.

Children's attachment to companion animals can also alleviate stress and anxiety, quell fears, and encourage academic and social development

for many struggling children. Being close to safe, attuned animals has physiological benefits, too. The act of petting an animal has been shown to lower blood pressure, and many people experience calmer breathing and a relaxed heart rate in the presence of a calm animal. It's no wonder many people seek out their pets when they feel upset and need comfort! Pets relieve stress and anxiety. Animals' "no-strings-attached" acceptance of a child's feelings offers a sense of love and acceptance—something that is so important in the early years and throughout life.

BUILDING VALUES

Another area scientists are beginning to explore is how animals help children develop their own values and morals. Empathy, compassion, and a sense of justice are innate qualities, part of what makes us human. We can look to children's interactions with animals to understand more deeply how children are demonstrating the development of many values, including caring (as discussed previously), empathy, and justice.

The World through Another's Eyes

Early relationships with animals help children develop empathy and other social competencies. *Empathy* is defined as "understanding, being aware of, being sensitive to, and vicariously experiencing the feelings, thoughts, and experience of another." Empathy involves considering the world from another's point of view. Often, it results in being able to put others' needs ahead of one's own. Being able to take the perspective of another creature, a separate "self," is a valuable aspect of children's development alongside animals. That the child is beginning to perceive that another creature has needs is the point, not whether the child's perceptions of an animal's needs are entirely accurate. When children feed pets, stroke them, brush them, and take care of them well, they are demonstrating and practicing empathy. If you watch a child interacting with a pet, she will demonstrate empathy by altering the way in which she pets the animal, speaks to it, and otherwise engages with it. She changes her behavior to respond to what she perceives the animal's feelings to be.

In this example, a five-year-old boy is holding a guinea pig on his lap:

> James: You are so nice, Ginger. Are you having a good day?
> *James strokes the guinea pig. Suddenly there is a loud banging clatter, as a child across the room drops a tray of wood blocks. The guinea pig jumps, startled.*
> James (*stroking her slowly, he quiets his voice to almost a whisper*): It's okay, Ginger. It's okay. That was just Charlie, he dropped the blocks. It's okay.

James's behaviors indicate a level of empathy for the guinea pig. First, he asked her if she was "having a good day," which indicates that he believed the guinea pig had feelings or an opinion about her day (as well as a shared concept of what a "day" is). Then, when the guinea pig was startled by the noise of the blocks, James recognized that the guinea pig had been startled, and he changed the tone of his voice, and he slowed the speed with which he was petting her in an effort to soothe her. He also reassured her about what was happening and told her that it was "okay." To do any of these things, the boy needed to imagine what the guinea pig was feeling. Some early childhood educators refer to this as "perspective taking."

Observing children's play behavior is another way that educators and parents can learn about children's perceptions and valuing of animals. Even their cognitive understanding of animals' behaviors as well as their physical needs is apparent in children's play. Adults may not realize the cognitive and empathetic skills involved in children's imitation of animals. But any group of preschoolers playing "kitties" on the playground demonstrates a distinct understanding of the animals' mannerisms, behavior, and typical responses:

> Mary: Meow, meow! (*She bats at a long ribbon dragged by Emma, who is walking past.*)
> Emma: Kitty, do you want to play? Do you like my ribbon?
> Zoe (*standing nearby*): Meow!
> *Zoe drops to all fours and scrambles over to Mary, batting at the ribbon with one hand. Emma walks and drags the ribbon, while Mary and Zoe follow on all fours, hopping and leaping after the ribbon.*

In this example, the two girls knew exactly how a pet cat would behave when taunted with a long ribbon. The cat would bat and paw at the ribbon and follow it. They expressed their excitement as human girls would do (by vocalizing), but since they had adopted cat personae, they used the language of cats to express their feelings. Emma, when speaking with the girls, used a higher-pitched tone of voice, as she might also do if she were talking to an infant. By taking on an animal's perspective, the children are demonstrating that they understand a wide range of behaviors and emotions. Children use their observational knowledge and playacting skills to demonstrate not only what they know but also their ability to empathize, to "put themselves in someone else's shoes." Playing at being animals can also offer children freedom to express more difficult emotions, such as anger or fear. Chapter 5 talks more about how you can encourage play behavior that supports children's growing understanding of animals and their feeling of connection to animals.

Another example shows how children can empathize with animals in and through specific social contexts:

At one outdoor play area, three boys are engaged in pretend play, acting out a scene where they are standing on a small hill, watching birds and playing in a fort, which is their "tepee." Another child assumes the role of the family dog, and the other children respond to him in kind, speaking to him in a special tone of voice reserved for the "dog," bringing him a dish of "treats" (pinecones and acorns), and inviting him on their "hunting trip."

Jack crawls toward the boys, barking and laughing. He moves toward the entrance of the fort.

Cole: He can be our dog.

Tyler: Yeah, but dogs stay outside.

Jack crawls out barking and whining. He goes away from the fort, pretends to lie down nearby.

Owen: Let's make the fort bigger, guys!

Jack, on all fours, comes back over, making barking and panting noises.

Lily (*to Jack*): Hey, boy, want a treat? (*She gives him a wood chip.*) I'll come over and give you a treat every day.

Owen (*to Lily*): This is our hunting house, no dogs allowed. There's a sign right there. (*Owen points to a sign in the play yard.*)

Lily: You can come with me, doggy. Dogs are allowed at my house. You're a good dog.

Jack barks, sits on haunches, moves front "legs" as if pawing at Lily, and rubs his cheek against her knee.

In this example, the child who was playing a dog demonstrated a perspective and knowledge of animal behavior by adopting its mannerisms (crawling on all fours, panting, sniffing at the "treats," cowering in a corner). Clearly this child was familiar with family dogs, and he was able to imitate how they act and respond. He knew that when dogs are scolded, they cower or shrink away from contact, and when praised, they respond with excitement and seek connection. In observing children's behavior when they are playacting at being animals, it is clear they have a strong grasp of the mannerisms and characteristics of animal behavior. They might be graceful deer bounding through a forest one moment, ferocious tigers stalking prey the next. Their physical behavior changes, their words and sounds change, and their movements adapt to better embody the creature they are playing.

These behaviors demonstrate cognitive development, because children are showing what they have learned about animal behavior through imitation. Through their playacting, the children are also developing empathy because they have to "see the world through the eyes of another" in order to imitate that animal. As children respond to one another in playacting, they are stretching their imaginary world. They are forced to imagine responses that would be consistent with the responses a dog or a cat would have. Chapter 5 has some ideas for deliberately helping to cultivate those feelings of empathy with animals. Empathy is an important skill to develop in early childhood. When children have empathy for animals, they also feel more empathy for other creatures, including humans.

Justice for All

Another important developmental milestone that can be observed in children is the emergence of a sense of justice. Most children, as mentioned earlier in the chapter, react with alarm or upset when they see or hear of an animal being harmed. Children recognize animals as living things and will defend them and take risks to ensure their well-being. Simply because they are living things, animals are valued by children, and therefore, children apply their newly developing sense of justice to animals. This moral concern arises naturally in early childhood, as during this time, children are also learning to be aware of fairness, rules, and cooperation and are practicing self-regulation (such as stopping oneself from doing something harmful or against the rules, even if "I really want to!").

Although much research still needs to be done, some researchers, such as Saunders and Myers, see it as "highly probable" that as children develop their cognitive awareness of animals and their needs, they develop a morality that involves caring about animals, which can lead to a sense of morality and care for habitats and ecosystems. This is a natural progression. Children learn that animals have unique and specialized needs, habitats, characteristics, and a place in a larger system. From this, a child's sense of caring and morality expands outward to include the natural world as he grows.

During a children's summer camp one afternoon, a group of children gather around a busy cluster of ants that had come across a melted ice cream sandwich. They watch with fascination as the ants mob the sugary stain on the sidewalk.

Drew, standing close to the ants, lifts his foot and stomps down hard, squashing dozens of ants.

Drew: Ha!

Several of the children scream. Mara is in tears and shrieking.

Patrick (*yelling and looking angry*): You killed them! You killed them!

Many of the children are visibly upset.

Mara (*crying*): They were alive, and now they're dead!

The children's knee-jerk reaction to the act of killing an animal, no matter how small, shows just how deeply children value animal life. The children didn't need to stop and think about the value of ants, their feelings about ants overall, or the role of ants in the school yard. They immediately felt upset at Drew's stomping on them. They felt it was wrong to kill the ants, simply because the ants were living things.

In many instances, there will be at least one or two children who seem to get a certain thrill from stomping on bugs, squashing caterpillars, or even screaming at the flock of pigeons on a sidewalk to watch them all flutter away in a panic. I've seen children become surprised and saddened when they realize they've accidentally killed a small creature. I've also seen them laugh with joy when they realize their own power—the sound of their voice scaring away a flock of birds or sending a squirrel scurrying up a tree. As a parent and educator, try to reserve judgment about the child's intentions. Avoid shaming the child. It's possible he's as upset as the other children. These are great opportunities to model compassion, kindness, and respect. If the child's actions are disturbing to you or to the other children, start a class discussion. Remind the children that it's always important to think about the effects of our actions and that we're a lot bigger than the tiny ants on the sidewalk and the squirrels out looking for an acorn to eat. Teach compassion, kindness, and respect in the classroom and outdoors through modeling.

The animal world influences the way children develop in a number of ways. Interactions with animals can teach children to differentiate the world of creatures, can help them learn caring for others, and can give them observational and relational skills. We can reasonably conclude that as children's cognitive understanding of animals' needs, characteristics, and place in the natural world grows, their love expands to include animals' ecosystems and the natural world as a whole. Educators and parents will do well by supporting children in deepening those relationships. When adults and caregivers offer a child opportunities to interact with animals, play at being animals, and care for animals, the child develops a sense of self, caring for others, relational skills, and ethics. Many children naturally seek out animal interactions. In doing so, they develop skills and values that will last them a lifetime.

Animals in Children's Everyday Lives

During a field trip to a local aquarium, a group of preschoolers sees a tank of tropical fish and searches excitedly for "Nemo"—a clown fish made popular by an animated movie.

During a family picnic, one five-year-old girl is terrified of getting stung by a bee. When asked about this, she tells her parents about a friend from school who is allergic to beestings. "My teacher says bees are bad news and can even kill some kids!" the girl reports.

A class of three-, four-, and five-year-olds arrives at a local nature center for a hike in the woods and a picnic. One four-year-old is afraid to get off the bus because he believes there are dinosaurs in the forest that will eat him.

All of these examples illustrate one point: children's prior knowledge of and experience with animals affect their perceptions of animals going forward. This chapter examines the state of most children's relationships with animals. Where do children encounter animals in their lives? How does the quality of children's experiences with animals influence their perceptions and expectations about animals? Educators and parents can evaluate children's interactions with animals to better understand children's relationships with animals and the implications for their development.

There are messages everywhere about how we relate to animals. Children are exposed to messages and interactions with animals in a range of settings, from family pets in the home to "wild" animals to popular books, games, and television shows. In every one of these contexts, young children are learning about animals. Through listening to adults' words and watching their behavior, children learn what to think and feel about animals, how to treat animals, and how to value animals. Because children carefully process and pick up on so much of our communication, both verbal and nonverbal, it's important for us as adults to be aware of the messages that we're sending.

ADULTS MODEL BEHAVIOR FOR CHILDREN

The adults in children's lives are their strongest models of behavior toward animals. Adults can provide or take away opportunities for interaction with animals, and they have the power to encourage or discourage children's expressed interests in animals. If adults are willing to help children identify and sort out their fears and misconceptions about animals, they can have a huge influence on how children behave toward animals. Adults also send messages about the role and value of animals in plenty of ways without ever opening their mouths.

Pets in the Home

In the United States, we spend billions of dollars every year on pets and pet supplies. In 2012, the total amount spent on pets approached $53 billion. Over 62 percent of households have at least one pet. Animals are important

to people, and these figures reflect that. Pets may range from goldfish to dogs and cats to reptiles, birds, or "pocket pets," such as hamsters or even ferrets. In other Western cultures, the trends are roughly the same. But across the world there are vast cultural differences in the ways that animals are regarded and treated. People from some cultures may scoff or raise their eyebrows at the high regard in which we hold our companion animals in North America. And it might seem strange to some people that certain species of animals, such as hedgehogs or crickets, are kept as pets in other cultures.

When children grow up with pets in the home and parents who express positive attitudes toward pets, they are more likely to feel interested in and enthusiastic about animals. Regardless of the amount of time a child spends with a pet at home, whether he or she "likes" the animal or participates directly in its care, that child is learning about

humans' relationships to animals. The words a child's parents or caregivers use when they speak about animals, the tones they use, and their demeanor toward the animals all teach a child about the value and role of animals in her family's life.

In a family where companion animals are held in high regard, and a strong level of attention and thought is given to the care and welfare of the animals, children will naturally adopt those feelings toward animals. When young children see their parents or caregivers being kind and receiving love and comfort from the presence of animals, they will naturally express the same behaviors and feelings toward those animals. And the teacher who is careful to speak gently to the classroom guinea pigs and always handles them carefully and calmly is teaching children a great deal about the kind of care that animals deserve. In homes and classrooms where treating animals with kindness, caring, and respect is normalized, children will adopt these behaviors. Even more importantly, children from homes with pets typically show more empathy to other children and adults, as well as to other animals.

Conversely, if a child is in a home where one parent likes fish, for example, and the other parent is indifferent and often forgets to feed them, the child may grow up with mixed feelings about fish and a sense that they are not as valuable to some people as to others. When a child sees his parent tenderly brushing the ears of his faithful old cocker spaniel each evening, he receives a different message than if he sees the dog teased or yelled at by the adults in the home—and it's not long before the child is doing the same. Perhaps a child is a member of a family or cultural group that believes "animals don't belong in a house." All of these situations are realistic. All of these situations contain many layers of meaning that children internalize.

In the wake of the tragic effects of Hurricane Katrina in 2005, the suffering of many New Orleans families was made worse by their separation from or loss of their beloved pets. In some cases, federal authorities had difficulty evacuating people who were unwilling to part with their animals, further complicating the disaster management. The widespread loss and suffering caused when families were separated from their pets spurred a nationwide overhaul of how pets are managed and cared for during natural disasters. Recognizing that a family's loss and trauma in a natural disaster are complicated by losing a pet, the Federal Emergency Management Association (FEMA) helped pass a law that provides financial assistance to states, cities, and towns for the safe evacuation and shelter of household companion animals in the event of a natural disaster. This became known as the Pet Evacuation and Transportation Standards Act of 2006, or the PETS act for short.

Educating Ourselves for Our Children

Some of the earliest lessons children learn about animals are modeled by the way that adults react to, respond to, talk about, and even communicate nonverbally with animals. Many adults respond to certain animals because of the messages they themselves received from a young age. Animals play such a wide variety of roles in our everyday lives that most people simply don't think about discussing their attitudes or value system toward animals. Perhaps you haven't even thought about it until now. It's enough to be aware of the many contexts and different places we find animals and to be prepared to discuss and examine them with children. But consider setting the stage for discussion and exploration of these subjects. As adults in our children's lives, we are responsible for our own value system and the ways we pass our values on.

The way that adults talk about and treat all animals, from beloved pets dressed in holiday sweaters to the spiders in the dusty corners of the basement, does not go unnoticed by children. Parents' language patterns (the words we use to describe animals or talk about them), facial expressions, tone of voice, and even body language can influence children's feelings about animals, even provoking fears or phobias in children. When the adults in a child's life openly disdain or fear a particular species, it follows that children will mirror and eventually share those feelings. (The bee at the family picnic at the beginning of the chapter is one example.) Simply put, if adults are fearful and uncomfortable with certain species of animals, children will be as well.

But the reverse is also true. Teachers who approach animals with care and curiosity can foster those feelings in children. One toddler teacher I know said, "I can't stand spiders! I really don't like them. But the children I work with don't know that, and they don't need to. I try to share their excitement even if I'm cringing on the inside. I just focus on the smiles on the children's faces instead of my own fears about spiders."

For young children, interpreting adults' communication about animals can at times be confusing. Consider this kindergarten classroom where the children are instructed by the teacher to "kill every ant you see; they don't belong inside!" while at home one girl's family has an attitude of compassion for animals that extends to even the smallest of creatures. At home all animals are treated with respect and care, while at school the teacher demonstrates disgust for certain species. A kindergarten-aged child will probably not consciously parse out this mixed message more deeply, but inner confusion is there: *What role does the ant actually have? Is this a creature to be respected or a creature I should kill without question? Why does my teacher want to kill this creature if my parents don't?* Feelings of anxiety, guilt, and confusion may result. Unfortunately, unless a savvy parent or teacher becomes aware of the differences between the values professed at home and those taught in the classroom, and is then prepared to explore them with the girl, she is left wondering.

Adults need to know what they personally believe before they can help children sort out feelings and impressions. Adults can help children by promoting interest and care according to their cultural values or even their desired values (for example, you may want children to appreciate and care about reptiles even if you yourself are a little bit squeamish about them). Animals are in many contexts and play many roles in our everyday lives, from companion animals, to insect "pests," to zoo animals, to the animals that provide the food on our plates, the shoes we wear, and the handbags we carry. All these contexts are opportunities to examine our values and explore them with children.

Sorting Our Categories

Another more subtle nonverbal message deals with the categories we assign animals to. Especially in early childhood settings, children and adults alike seem to naturally put animals into certain groups, depending on our perceptions of differences, such as where those animals live or their roles in humans' lives. While the logic and nuances of how animals are fit into their particular categories are not scientific or explicit, these categories make a certain amount of intuitive sense. Although I caution against using categories too specifically when thinking about animals' value and roles, identifying them can help us see the parameters of our own shared understanding. When colleagues refer to "farm animals," for example, you probably have a general sense of what animals they're referring to. Consider the following categories of animals and the values they may emphasize.

Farm Animals Consider the types of animals shown in one early childhood classroom. In the dramatic play area, there is a wooden barn and an assortment of small plastic animals including pigs, goats, sheep, horses, cows, and chickens. Ask any child what these creatures have in common, and most will tell you that these are "farm animals." In the minds of many children, these animals are all characters that live on the imagined "farm" setting. In reality, the animals in this category are most commonly used for food. That food might be meat, or it might be eggs, milk, or another product that we obtain through the husbandry of the animal. These animals may have also been associated historically with farming because they served a role in creating farms, such as by pulling plows, milk wagons, and so on.

While many young children are probably not ready to understand a category called "food animals," many educators agree that children should be made aware of the animal origins of many of the foods we consume, at a developmentally appropriate level, of course. Some children who have more experience with farming or animal husbandry (perhaps through their own rural upbringing or programs like 4-H) will be more familiar with the notion that animals do provide us with food. To other children, this may be a new idea. While the issue of raising animals for food is a difficult one for many people to acknowledge, much less address in the early childhood classroom, the reality is that much of our food comes from animals. We eat their meat; we get eggs, milk, yogurt, and other products from them. Honey is produced by bees. And many beneficial insects are responsible for pollinating the trees and plants that give us many of our favorite fruits. This

information can be gently conveyed to children in the early childhood setting in ways such as by simply telling stories about how bees and other pollinators do their work.

Our categories also show a measure of value. Farm animals, for example, are valued in our culture mainly because they produce things like meat, eggs, honey, leather, and wool. The products we obtain from these animals are important to our diet, economy, convenience, and comfort. While all children (and adults) may not be ready to dive into a discussion of animal value, this is something to think about. Our many toys, songs, and stories about farm animals are an opportunity to provide information to children about where food comes from—and to do it in a way that is sensitive, thoughtful, compassionate, and developmentally appropriate.

Pets in the Home As a category, pets usually include the familiar cats, dogs, gerbils, guinea pigs, goldfish, and other common household companion animals. This category, perhaps more than the others, varies widely depending on cultural beliefs about animals and their place in the home. In some cultures, for example, dogs simply do not belong in the home; in other cultures, dogs are the most common household pets. In some settings, the idea of keeping a snake in a tank as a family (or classroom) pet may be abhorrent. In other settings, it's perfectly valid. Some children keep countless number of critters they find outside as short-term pets. Others might regard horses or other "working animals" as pets. Many children will have different definitions based on their own pets and their own experiences with friends', neighbors', and relatives' pets. Again, there are many gray areas with these categories.

Zoo Animals Ask a group of five-year-olds to list "zoo animals," and you'll likely hear about monkeys, elephants, giraffes, hippos, rhinos, alligators, and many more. This category includes animals that most children have likely not ever seen in the wild but have possibly seen in zoos and also in books and as toys. This category includes animals considered to be "exotic" or native to regions far from where the children are located. Some children

might also include captive animals, such as those found in nature centers, in this category. Which animals children (and adults) assign to this category depends in large part on the animals they've encountered in zoos. Children might also draw on their experience with aquariums and zoos to create a category of "sea animals," which includes animals found throughout the world's oceans, such as whales, dolphins, octopuses, tropical fish, sea horses, jellyfish, and eels. Children who live near the ocean and have a firsthand understanding of this environment will likely have a much wider (and more accurate) list of animals that belong in this category.

Again, the labels we use often influence our perception of value. Animals we call "zoo" animals may be valued by our culture because they entertain and intrigue us. Organizations that exist to house and support these animals are important to the economic climate of the cities and states in which they exist. In many cases zoos and other animal-related destinations are involved in important education and conservation efforts worldwide. Cute "zoo" animal images adorn everything from soda cans to children's pajamas to tote bags. Corporations and even nonprofit organizations value these animals partly because of their ability to captivate the hearts and minds of people, to tug at their heartstrings.

Other animals, such as rare or endangered wild animals, are considered by some people to have obvious intrinsic value; that is, they are valued simply because they exist, regardless of their role in humans' lives. Many people don't even need to see or ever encounter a very rare animal to hold it in high esteem. While young children may not be aware of an animal's relative scarcity or its status as endangered or threatened, children do pick up on adults' attitudes about these animals.

Wild Animals The animals in this category will vary quite a bit depending on where you live, but, in the words of one boy, these animals "roam free and live outside." For some people, this category might also include the

captive animals exhibited at nature centers and natural history museums. Others may lump carnivores such as lions and bears into this category, preferring to define as "wild" those animals that have achieved something of a celebrity status in our culture.

Creepy Crawlies Another common category that people may identify is "scary" or "yucky" animals. In this category, children and adults may include insects, spiders, reptiles, amphibians, and other less-than-cute animals with which they are familiar. Often these animals take center stage around the Halloween holiday, as many children and adults alike consider them scary or ominous. This category will have lots of variation, and my guess is that the family of each child in your program has different lists for each of these categories. You may, too!

In many cases, animals that fall into the "creepy crawly" or pest category are given little respect or consideration. Many people think it's a moral right to kill or destroy any animal whose behavior conflicts with the interest of humans. A raccoon who seeks shelter in a chimney stack may well be considered a pest and disposed of. In the wild, however, that same raccoon wandering across a hiking trail might give a family a thrill they'll remember forever—an encounter with a wild animal. Insects such as ants, wasps, and beetles are often exterminated without a second thought. Insects seem to be the most "disposable" of all animals, as evidenced by the simple fact that many people do not hesitate to kill them when the insects' behaviors conflict with human comfort, safety, or convenience.

In other cultures, the categories may vary, and the animals may experience different treatment than those in Western culture do. In some cultures, for example, cows are sacred and wander freely through the city. Crickets and other insects are kept as pets in fancy cages.

Why is it necessary to identify and understand these categories? For one thing, it helps us recognize that we may assign animals different qualities and standards of treatment and regard based on which categories they fall into. This is neither right nor wrong; it simply is. The point of identifying these categories is to see how we naturally assign certain animals to certain categories. While those categories are not necessarily scientific or even logical, they are there. Consciously or not, to some degree we all assign animals to those categories, and recognizing that can help us understand others' and our own perceptions of animals.

Of course no child has a life where all adults share the same philosophy about all things. Differences in ethics, priorities, and worldview are what makes this world such a diverse and interesting place. But identifying and discussing those differences, as well as exploring our own feelings, values, and motivations behind those differences, can put a child on a path to understanding her own feelings about animals and the place she creates in her own world for them.

ANIMALS' PORTRAYALS IN MEDIA

Media are a huge part of childhood. Books, toys, games, television programs, movies—and animal characters—play a large role in children's lives. Think for a moment about all the children's television programs that feature animals as main characters.

Animals portrayed in the media are almost always animal characters with anthropomorphized characteristics. *Anthropomorphism* is the attribution of human characteristics, behaviors, or physical traits to nonhumans. (In children's media, not only animals but also plants and objects such as machines and vehicles are frequently anthropomorphized.) An example of anthropomorphism is portraying a monkey that has long eyelashes, wears a dress, carries a purse, talks, and drives a car to the mall, where she takes her five children (also monkeys) shopping for school clothes.

Anthropomorphism of animals is not necessarily a bad thing—it can be useful in helping children process feelings and thoughts. It can engage children and pique their curiosity. It can even help to ignite interest in real-life animals. Animals that have human characteristics can help children relate to them and their story. Portrayals of animals having anxiety about their first day of school, having disputes with friends, and having nightmares can alleviate children's own concerns and let them know that their feelings are shared—they aren't alone. Moreover, having an animal model these behaviors allows children to immediately identify with the character. If a character in a book is a Caucasian male child, many other children may feel "that's not me" when they hear the story and see the pictures. If the character is a goose, however, its very differentness allows all children to identify with the inherent similarities. The storybook goose is happy, sad, scared, or hurt, and children can identify with these generic similarities without having to address other social issues. Popular children's books that address difficult topics such as major life transitions, traumas, and other challenging situations often feature animals as characters. Anthropomorphized animals can help children overcome potential barriers because they relate easily to the animals in a playful way that keeps their interest.

However, giving human characteristics to animals can also complicate and confuse the issues surrounding children's relationships to animals. The animal stereotypes created in storytelling—and even the act of storytelling itself—have a potential impact on the way children view animals. This impact may be both positive and negative. While this doesn't mean telling animal stories is wrong, it is something to be aware of and think about.

Books, Toys, and Children's Environments

Animals play a prominent role in children's books, toys, and games. In a survey, a researcher looked at animals and the natural world portrayed in over one thousand fiction and nonfiction children's books. Most of the books featured animals as main characters. The majority of animals featured in these books were domestic animals such as cats, dogs, and other pets or farm animals. When wild animals were portrayed, they were rarely found in their natural habitats. In many of these books, animals didn't behave like animals at all—they possessed very human characteristics including wearing clothes, attending school, and struggling with the same issues that many human children face. While some are chagrined by the lack of scientific accuracy in children's literature, there is no denying that many children's books contain beautiful illustrations that capture children's imaginations, inspire interest, and support a child's aesthetic sensibility. Though some storybook portrayals of animals are not scientifically accurate by any means, they do serve a valuable function. They can engage children more deeply in the stories, promote language acquisition, and build emotional investment in the stories.

Any casual trip to a toy store will show that children love playing with animals, too. Stuffed animals, plastic and wooden figures, and stylized animals

fill a child's world of toys. For better or for worse, sets featuring groups or collections of animals encourage children to acquire a great number of species or individuals of a species, such as the popular Littlest Pet Shop toys and Calico Critters. The educational value of these toys could be called in to question, as some toy manufacturers do a better job than others of representing the animals accurately, but then again, not all toys are intended to be scientifically accurate representations!

The wide variety of animal toys ranges from hand-carved wooden "natural" toys to dress-up ponies with interchangeable hairstyles and princess gowns. I have seen creatures no bigger than a kidney bean in every species imaginable—all with big eyes and wispy hair atop their tiny heads. Others, aimed at boys, range from robotic hamsters dressed in military camouflage, complete with machine gun sound effects, to vehicle-animal hybrids and spherical electronic warrior animals that are designed to "fight" one another in a plastic arena. Perhaps due to a lack of marketing dollars, a lack of connection to television characters, or something else, toys that realistically portray animals make up a relatively small percentage of the toy market in the United States. Again, it's not within the scope of this book to analyze toy trends with any depth. I'll leave it to the reader to consider why that might be, but it bears mention. Many realistic animal toys, both plastic and wooden, are also available. Many early childhood supply companies offer collections of wildlife and ocean animals native to certain regions of the United States or other countries.

In addition to filling the bookshelves and the toy box, animals are depicted on children's clothing and bedding, backpacks and lunchboxes, sippy cups and bottles, hats and mittens, bikes and trikes, potty chairs, strollers, buckets, tools, bedroom decorations, and more. A recent walk through the children's section at my local "big box" store yielded over 350 children's products depicting animals. And that was just the children's section. I didn't venture into the books and media, clothing, bedding, or sporting goods areas. Marketers have long understood that including a well-regarded animal on a product can stimulate interest and boost sales. Animals are especially interesting for children and are often used as a means to get children's attention. It's no surprise: animals are compelling for people of all ages. We know that children and adults alike respond favorably to photos and images that contain animals—such as the many political pictures that include "the family dog" and photos of famous people and their pets. Many children's products (such as clothing and bedding) remain in the backdrop of a child's life. But toys, games, and books are often in the forefront—they take up a lot of space in a child's bedroom as well as a child's mind.

Screen Media

Screen media are another context with countless examples and portrayals of animals. Animals star in many of the most popular children's movies and television programs, and this has been true since the early days of television and movies. Many popular movies aimed at young children feature animals as main characters. Video games, educational "apps," and other computer programs featuring animals abound. Although main animal characters range from domestic collies and dolphins to cartoon robotic animals and pets that talk and create flying machines, the fact remains that they are all animal representations—and they still have wide appeal for children.

Screens Are Everywhere Children Are

Screen media are so much a part of American culture that many adults hardly recognize their prevalence, especially in children's lives. The National Association for the Education of Young Children has clear guidelines about media consumption (see appendix A, Additional Resources, for a link to its joint position paper on screen time). Recent research estimates the total television time for children under age eleven at approximately twenty-five hours per week (not including computers, video games, and other screen time). The American Academy of Pediatrics reports that by age three, about one-third of American children have televisions in their rooms. The television is known as the "electronic babysitter" for good reason—turn it on and children are transfixed. Parents often use the television to provide themselves with a much-needed break to get dinner started or work on their own projects at home, or to quiet whining children. And many a busy parent passes a child a cell phone loaded with apps or video games to distract an impatient child in the line at the supermarket. Computers and other digital media purport to offer a host of educational benefits for children, and eager parents aim to help prepare their preschoolers for academic life by offering screen-based "learning games." Once children reach school age, many of them enter environments where at least some time is spent each day in front of a screen, even just computer stations and iPads.

Not only do children view screen media frequently, but the intensity of their interactions with television, movies, video games, apps, and the like means that they also absorb far more of it than adults may realize. It's important to be aware of the ways animals are portrayed in children's media so that you can help children sort out the messages they receive about animal relationships, behavior, and roles. This is not to imply that you should expect scientifically accurate information about animals to be present in all children's media, nor that you need to police their intake strictly. But few educators and parents would disagree with the need to be involved and participate in children's media consumption, and this involvement includes being aware of how animals are represented.

Animals Are Everywhere, Too

In this maelstrom of screen time, then, consider how often animals are featured. Scores of computer games and apps feature animals as the main characters. "Educational" software programs designed to help children read or practice their math or keyboarding skills often feature animals as characters, coaches, or "avatars"—characters that children can name and label and that represent the child online while she is engaged in a computer game. Because of the wide appeal that animals have, children's television programs often feature animals as main characters. Children's cartoons, live-action series, and documentary programs (and, of course, advertisements aimed at children) all feature animals. Children's programs feature exotic and common animal species, and some even feature creatures that resemble animals more than humans but aren't recognizable as any species yet known!

These multitudes of animal characters and situations in screen media can be both entertaining and misleading. Depictions of animals are rarely realistic, and, more often than not, they are stylized and made fantastic through anthropomorphism. For example, we find portrayals of animals that are not accurate—their bodies may be misshapen, or they may have human characteristics or wear clothes. They may be out of context, or they may occur in settings with disparate species that would never coexist in the "real world"—for example, hippos frolicking with domestic cats. Animals are often portrayed doing things that animals in the real world do not do—riding bicycles, for example, or flying planes. Animals that rarely encounter each other in the wild may be pitted against each other or portrayed as "enemies."

Again, I'm not saying that all media to which children are exposed should be scientifically accurate. I simply bring this to your attention to increase awareness of the many portrayals animals receive in media.

Animal Characters with Kid-Sized Problems

Chapter 3 alluded to the ways living animals can help children process their feelings. Animal characters in media can do so as well, albeit in different ways. Media images and stories can help children identify, express, and understand their feelings. Children may recognize qualities they possess in animal characters, or they may vicariously experience their own fantasies about life through the characters. Consider, for example, the legions of young girls who love the television program and stories featuring a young mouse who attends a fancy ballet school. The mouse is an early elementary student, and she endures many of the same struggles that young human girls feel. She gets into squabbles with her friends, she has to do household chores, she has occasional problems in school, and she feels jealous or afraid at times, too. Children may see themselves mirrored in characters who have the same problems they themselves do, and observing with "emotional distance" how the animal characters resolve heavy problems can be therapeutic. On the other hand, the mouse in these stories also reinforces some stereotypes about girls and the behavior that is expected of them, such as the desire to wear fancy dresses, a competitive attitude with peers, and a tendency to worry and fuss over physical appearance.

Children's stories that feature animals as the main characters are often successful in bypassing barriers to understanding by using a character that children can immediately relate to. Perhaps this is why so many beloved children's books feature animals as main characters. In the beloved children's story *The Kissing Hand* the character who's nervous about leaving Mommy for the start of school is a young raccoon. Children of both genders can easily relate to this character. Since the main character is an animal, the character overcomes any immediate relational barrier. If the character in this story were a Caucasian boy, over half the potential audience would be left out. Many children would feel "he's not like me" and would therefore be unable to relate to the character as directly as they do to an animal. When the character is an animal, the barrier of "like me/not like me" has already been overcome. It is actually easier for the child to identify with the character for the very reason that it is so different from the child herself.

There are many contexts and characters in which children can see their own inner fears, hopes, worries, and dreams played out on the screen in animal form. Children may project their own feelings and "inner struggles" onto the animal characters they see on the programs they watch and the stories they hear. This is perhaps one reason that animals make such popular, approachable, and endearing subjects for children.

In many ways, animals can also serve as "blank slates" onto which children can project superhuman or special powers that they would like to have. A popular children's cartoon portrays a pet platypus who is also a top-secret spy. His human owners are blissfully unaware, all the while thinking their pet is an average platypus. But the character embodies the reserved, solitary, and awkward characteristics many young children see in themselves, and it's only in secret that he, and perhaps they, can unleash superpowers.

When children experience media with adults who engage them in thoughtful observation and awareness, they can develop analytical skills while they're learning about animals. Children's interest in animals can be used to involve them in valuable storytelling with animal characters. Unfortunately, the media can also misinform, misrepresent, and even mislead children (and adults!). Unless programs and other media are consumed with a critical eye and thoughtful discussion, children passively consume stories, images, and ideas with no opportunity to process, decode, or sort out the feelings they provoke. Simply put, very young children are ill equipped to make many distinctions between what's "real" and what's "not real" on television. They lack skills of discernment and deserve to have an adult's help to process and understand what they are seeing. While most children will recognize by the age of two or three that, say, hamsters do not wear clothes and fly homemade airplanes, when we expose them to these portrayals of animals with no discussion or examination, we do both children and animals a disservice. For example, if a child has only ever seen cartoons where foxes are mean and ruthless, how is he to know how foxes behave in real life? What expectations does this create? As adults who care for children, we are obliged to evaluate whether the media they are exposed to are developmentally appropriate, whether they accurately and fairly portray other living creatures and ecosystems, and how (or if) they serve our children's best interests.

Stereotypes on the Screen

Of course, not all media are intended to provide scientifically accurate information about animals. Recognizing this, adults should critically examine the information children are receiving about animals. Just being aware of the portrayals of animals and discussing that or pointing it out with children can be the first step to an ongoing, thoughtful examination of animal images in the media. What roles and stereotypes do we see animals play in children's media? Children can see animals playing the role of hero, community helper, villain, victim, student, and protagonist, all before breakfast.

What You See Is (More Than) What You Get Picture a cartoon shark. Chances are the image in your mind has mean-looking eyes, a stern expression, and a wide grin full of very sharp teeth. The way animals are portrayed in media often allows children to predict their personalities, and that predictability can be comforting to children. One never knows which child on the playground will wind up bullying others, or which teacher in school will be the grumpy one who's having a bad day. Humans' faces and body language rarely belie their personalities or demeanors. As I overheard one kindergartener say to another, "You look like you're nicer than you are…"

When it comes to animal characters, refreshingly, what you see is what you get. In many movies, animals are both heroes and villains, and the villains are ugly, powerful, and mean. Some animals are drawn to look especially sinister: long, sharp teeth, or red eyes, or shadowy skin. Frequently we see snakes, bears, sharks, and other predators depicted as the "bad guy," and their appearance belies their personality.

Other physical characteristics may be exaggerated, too. Giraffes and horses may have extremely long, thin legs or necks. Fish lips are excessively pronounced. Dogs' tongues wag and flap. Cats' claws and sharp teeth are exaggerated, and their slim bodies weave and slither. Many "goofy sidekick" characters resemble the stereotypical southern bumpkin, complete with buckteeth, crossed eyes, and gangly limbs. Some even have accents.

The popular program *Dora the Explorer* features a crafty fox who causes trouble and is best avoided. He reinforces the common stereotype that foxes are sneaky and sly and up to no good. We see this stereotype again and again in beloved fairy tales, myths, and legends spanning cultures, generations, and ages that feature animals like foxes and coyotes plotting to trick humans and other animals for their own benefit.

In many cases, the stereotypes and fearful portrayals of animals can be difficult for young children to process. Thus, these portrayals further reinforce the anxiety that some children may feel about animals. Consider: if the only exposure a child has to snakes is seeing them portrayed as ugly, sinister, and evil, how is the child to react when confronted with a real snake? What expectations will the child have?

Familiar Animals In many popular children's fairy tales, television programs, and movies, an animal serves the role of a helper or "familiar" (a helpful animal companion) who assists the main character in achieving the outcome that will bring about a happy ending. In the animated movie of Rudyard Kipling's *The Jungle Book*, Mowgli is vulnerable and lonely without his companion Baloo the Bear. Alice has her White Rabbit, who helps her navigate her way through Wonderland; Dorothy has her faithful and everlasting source of comfort, Toto. The role of the "animal familiar" reinforces the idea promoted in fairy tales the world over: animals can be your helper, your guide, and your friend. I'm not advocating for complete scientific accuracy in cartoons and games, but it is worthwhile to consider the impact of the imagery and caricatures of animals that children absorb.

Male Roles: Strong, Distant, and Powerful The messages children receive from animals' gender roles in media can be powerful. Heroes are usually portrayed as strong, confident, easygoing, swarthy, and competent males. Cartoon villains are also usually male, with big, strong bodies and deep voices. Males rarely nurture less powerful characters—that's the job of the females. When they do play the role of caretaker or nurturer, they are often used as a means to poke fun at males' supposed lack of ability in caring for young. Consider the example of Pongo, the father dog in *101 Dalmatians*. Pongo is a rare example of a nurturing father in the media, but when left alone with his babies, he has his paws full and can't keep the pups from spilling paint, messing the kitchen, and getting into other mischief.

In many children's movies, the role of the father is to teach the young son to fight, be strong, and strike out on his own. When male characters show fear or cry—if they cry at all—it's often to provide comic relief and or to portray a failure or weakness of the character. The role of the male character is usually to overcome his own vulnerability or weakness (think of the lost lion cub in Disney's *The Lion King*). Through their trials, male characters typically confront and overcome an enemy through an intense power struggle (usually through physical aggression that is graphic and violent) and triumph, demonstrating prowess and physical strength. Male television characters may not go through the same "Hero's Journey," but they often do share the same physical characteristics and personality characteristics just described. Or, as in the case of *Arthur* (a show about a smart aardvark who wears glasses), characters may be portrayed as intelligent but also socially awkward, a bit of a misfit. Even if they are protagonists, these "brainiac" characters are often the butt of many jokes.

These media portrayals provide boys and girls alike with one view of how males are "supposed" to look, act, and feel in the face of struggle and conflict. They also tell them something about the value of intelligence and its relation to social success. It would seem that children absorb from these programs a sense that males are aggressive, powerful, and independent but not nurturing. Males don't depend on others, and they aim to be the best. Of course, these are just examples—not all children will take these messages to heart, and not all messages are this overt.

Female Roles: Sweet, Supportive, and Sexualized Similarly, many female animal characters play certain stereotyped roles. In some movies, such as the popular *Finding Nemo,* Dory, the main female character, exists mainly to help the male character and to be the butt of the jokes. She fills the role of "dumb but lovable sidekick," which is ubiquitous in children's movies.

In many children's movies and television, female animal characters are docile, their main purpose being to make the male characters appear stronger or more powerful. Consider Faline in Disney's *Bambi*, Maid Marian in Disney's *Robin Hood*, and the mother cat in *The Aristocats.* These characters often need help or coaching from males. Their primary role is to help the males achieve their goals. When the characters are companions to humans (such as the animal companions in *Cinderella, The Little Mermaid*, and *Sleeping Beauty*), their role is often to provide beauty advice or help the main character with courtship, fashion, or hair challenges.

In many popular television programs aimed at young children, female animal characters struggle with relationships, and they deal with many of the same issues that human teenagers deal with. They are jealous and petty and in fierce competition with one another for attention and popularity. Their interests are often limited to clothes, fashion, jewels, and popularity. In one program, a pony who is a baker eats and demonstrates a voracious appetite, while other ponies tease her and make disparaging remarks about her weight and body. Although several of the ponies in this program have super-powers, much of their magic energy is used to create jewels and material goods for themselves, to make themselves more beautiful, or to outwit or compete with one another. Rarely do the female characters collaborate with each other or help one another. What does this tell young girls about what's important and how to be successful?

In subtle, and sometimes not-so-subtle, ways, many female cartoon animals are drawn with sexual features such as long eyelashes, pouty lips, round, pert bottoms, and even hints of cleavage. Female animal characters who wear clothes often sport bikinis, short skirts, or tight dresses. They may wear high-heeled shoes and even sport accessories such as handbags, hair ornaments, and jewelry. I've seen sexualized animal characters even featured in programs or as toys for a target audience as young as three years old. The behavior of these characters also reinforces harmful ideas about girls' roles. Female animals may assume docile, passive behaviors, which strengthen the male animals' personae. To many children and adults, these features are subtle and may go unnoticed.

These examples offer further support for adults supervising a child's television viewing. In many cases, simple questions such as, "Do you think that's what horses really look like?" or "She doesn't seem to know much about what to do. How would you solve that problem?" can help children reflect on the images and personalities they see portrayed by their favorite animal characters.

Like it or not, children do identify with animal characters. Overall, children's programs do little to further children's self-images or views of themselves as competent, helpful, cooperative problem solvers. Because children often identify on a conscious and subconscious level with the characters they watch, it's important for adults to critically evaluate what they're seeing. When young girls see themselves reflected in petty characters who argue about clothes and jewelry, and aspire to be popular above all else, and young boys identify with aggressive characters who fight to get to the top, they may approach their own relationships influenced by these behaviors. Television is not intended to boost children's self-esteem or teach them life lessons, but most educators, pediatricians, and child development experts agree: children do respond to the subtle messages and communications offered by television programs and movies. They learn certain things and internalize messages from programs and movies, whether we like that or not.

Animals playing anthropomorphized roles can often lead to unrealistic stereotypes. Not only are these kinds of portrayals potentially harmful to children's self-images, understanding of gender roles, and sexuality, but they can also be harmful to a child's developing understanding of animals' roles in ecological systems and authentic animal behavior. And children's capacity to sort out the "real" from the "not real" on television is still imma-ture, so it's important to talk honestly about animal characters and ways they are portrayed. Ask children questions about what they see. Listen to their observations and the conclusions they make. And have a discussion with them. Chances are, children will welcome the opportunity to talk with any adult who's interested in having a conversation about their favorite cartoon characters!

Reality Documentaries

Educators and parents often fall into the trap of thinking "documentary" pro-gramming or "reality-based" television shows are educational in nature and will provide accurate portrayals of animals in their natural environments, acting in ways that are natural and normal for them. In reality, many of these programs reinforce stereotypes or misinformation as well. Young children have trouble differentiating the "realistic" from the "overly dramatized" content on documentary programs. Again, it's important to view programs together and discuss the content.

In an effort to grab viewers' attention, some "nature" programs may por-tray animals such as lions and other predators as hungry, sinister, and overly aggressive animals, constantly on the prowl, dominating the environment in which they live. Or they show animals engaged in constant battles or life-or-death scenarios, with the constant threat of predators looming and other intraspecies dramas being played out. Narration includes a great deal of anthropomorphism as well—attributing human wants and needs to the animals in the films and voicing human expectations and interpretations. In reality, the life of an elephant may be quite boring from a child's perspective, consisting of several hours of walking and foraging each day. Some of the programs featured on the "nature" channels are documentaries, but others are what I term "sensationalized documentaries." These programs tend to glamorize or vilify animals and their natural behaviors in the interest of creating exciting, dramatic programs. While this approach certainly makes for exciting viewing, it does portray animals' lives and behavior in a way that may be somewhat exaggerated for the sake of drama. This can be a disservice to children because it creates misunderstanding by glamorizing animal behavior. On the other hand, these documentaries can also offer exciting opportunities for children to see real animals doing things that they would likely never be able to witness in real life.

The sense of danger and intensity that comes from this kind of programming can also be stressful for children. In an effort to increase interest, producers may show the subjects of their programs as constantly on the move, hiding from predators, seeking out other animals of the same species, and fighting for their lives. In many programs, baby or young animals are pursued, preyed upon, or made orphans when their animal parent is eaten or killed. One movie I recently saw portrayed a cat and two dogs falling into a river and being rushed over a waterfall. This sort of thing can be extremely upsetting for some children. Remember that young children often unconsciously project themselves onto media characters, so when a baby polar bear is stranded on an ice floe with no mother or a baby seal is pursued by a hungry killer whale, in effect, some children are experiencing the events themselves very intensely on a psychological level. Further, seeing an animal in a live-action situation where the animal appears to be in danger can also be very upsetting. Regardless of how many times an adult reminds him the movie is "just pretend," a young child does not realize how movies are made, and the adult must remember how real these things can seem.

One five-year-old boy was despondent after seeing a children's live-action movie with a fictional story where a wolf got "killed." He didn't understand that the wolf was an actor responding to training by "pretending to die" and that it had not really died. No amount of discussion could assuage his anxiety. He simply couldn't erase the scary image from his mind of the wolf "dying." This is another reason to consider the developmental stages of young children when offering media. Movie, television, and video game ratings are set by organizations that use criteria such as the amount of profanity, sexual language, and violence in a program or movie. By these standards, the content in the example above would be perfectly appropriate: there was no profanity, sexual language, or human violence in the movie, after all. Many people who care for children understand that there are plenty of other criteria by which to judge whether a program is appropriate. Taking into account the unique feelings, sensitivities, fears, curiosities, and personalities of young children, educators and parents can make individual decisions about whether certain documentary programming is appropriate (or not) for the children in their care.

Sensationalized documentaries can also set up unrealistic expectations for how animals behave.

In one summer camp program, children (ranging in age from four to twelve) are playing in the woods when they see a large black beetle ambling up a tree. Farther up the trunk an insect called a cicada killer is clinging to the wood.

The children watch the insects with attention for a few short moments.

Jace: Whoa! They're gonna have a battle!

Deon: Kill! Kill each other!

Henry (*pointing at the cicada killer*): Go on man, get him!

Jace: They are gonna kill each other! Fight, fight! (*Jace pokes at the beetle with a stick. The beetle scrambles farther up the tree.*)

Deon: Now they will fight!

Jace: Come on buggy boy, do something!

The boys clearly expect some drama much like the sorts of animal interactions they've come to expect from documentaries and other programs. Despite the children's cheering and urgings, the insects go about their own business, oblivious to each other. After a few minutes of waiting for the insects to "do something," the children grow bored and move on to other activities.

Somehow, the insects' natural behaviors weren't exciting enough to warrant more than a few distracted moments of the children's attention. When they realized the insects weren't going to engage in an epic battle or do something equally dramatic, they simply lost interest. If shown on television, the interaction between two gruesome-looking insects almost certainly would have been matched by dramatic music, narration, and conflict. Unfortunately for the summer campers, these insects had no apparent interest in each other and were busy doing their own things. Children can easily develop unrealistic expectations about how animals behave in the wild. Who wants to watch a squirrel simply scurry from branch to branch? Educators need to help children find the joy in simple, everyday events if we are going to help our children connect more deeply with animals. This can be encouraged simply through providing children opportunities to get outdoors, experiencing the natural world where all sorts of animals go about their daily lives.

Helping Children Think through Media

As adults who care for children, it's important to be aware of depictions of animals, their humanized selves, their behavior, and their relationships so that we can help children identify and sort them out. Given the great deal of time children spend with media, which likely will continue to increase as more and more apps and programs are brought to market, we need to recognize the role it has in shaping children's perceptions of animals, and by extension, themselves. Again, I'm not suggesting that you remove all cartoon images of animals or ban playthings that are overtly stereotypical (although these approaches may feel appropriate to you). I simply suggest several things:

- Become aware of the nuances and layers of meaning that children are presented by electronic media. They are told a great deal about animals, and by extension about themselves, when they passively consume media. I encourage educators and parents to use these "teachable moments" to parse out the meaning in children's programming. What are the ways in which female animal characters are portrayed in your child's favorite program? Which animals are represented? What behaviors are animals used to personify? What personality traits? Which animals represent the "good guys" and the "bad guys"? Talk with children. Ask them for their opinions and impressions. Discuss the tools that the animators use to help communicate the character's personality, such as using red eyes and sharp teeth to portray mean characters.

- Consider consumption patterns. How are animals depicted on the items in your classroom, in your child's bedroom, or on your bookshelf? Is there a wide range of images, or are they all licensed-and-merchandised characters? Do children have a chance to see animals portrayed in lots of different ways? Introduce variety where you can, or cull some of the unrealistic images of animals from the shelves. Make diversity a high priority. Provide a variety of depictions of animals to spark curiosity and conversation.

- Have intentional conversations about media together. Ask children if the characters they see are doing realistic things. Find out what they know about real animals. Ask how images and characters make them feel. Talk about how animals in books and media are interacting with one another. Use their natural interest and curiosity that's spawned by animals in media to learn more about certain animals through books and other formats.

Again, an outright ban on media may not be practical or appropriate, but consider including more accurate portrayals as well. Seek out realistic animal images in programs and video games. Find toys that are relatively realistic in shape and color, rather than only offering brightly colored, clothed animal toys. When children are exposed to media in the presence of an engaged adult, media images and stories can also help children develop important thinking skills, such as making observations, asking questions, drawing conclusions, and making predictions. Media can excite, inform, provoke, and arouse interest in new subjects or familiar ones. Television programs portraying animals can be comforting, exciting, and stimulating experiences for children, all of which are opportunities for learning, growth, and just plain fun!

ANIMALS IN THE "WILD"

Fortunately, many children's experience of nature does go beyond the animal documentaries on television. A trip to a local park, a picnic in the school yard, and even a walk through the neighborhood will offer young children plenty of exciting opportunities to see common and abundant wild creatures. Educators who work with young children know that it doesn't take a large, charismatic mammal to spark a child's interest. Young children are delighted by virtually any real animal they encounter outdoors, be it an ant on the sidewalk or a garter snake sunning itself on the asphalt in the parking lot.

This is good news, because most large animals tend to stay away from human habitation and are difficult to see outdoors. In some areas of my home state, Minnesota, large mammals such as white-tailed deer and even moose have adapted to living close to humans and may occasionally be seen. In other areas, coyotes, foxes, and raccoons aren't unusual. But in most urban areas, children are most likely to have encounters with common backyard birds, ducks and geese, squirrels, and insects such as ants, bees, and butterflies. And often, these small and familiar critters are just as exciting to a child.

Seeing animals in nature often becomes a child's treasured memory. Since "wild" animals live outdoors, they have special qualities that make them that much more exciting to children: Their homes are different than ours. They have to find their own food. They have special powers (flying, climbing to the tops of trees, digging holes), and in most cases, they choose when to be seen by children—not the other way around.

A rabbit hops across a grassy patch outside a classroom window, and the children in the classroom come undone. They crowd the glass and do their very best to speak in hushed voices:

> Dionne: A bunny! (*He presses his face to the glass and watches.*)
>
> Charlie (*in a stage whisper*): He's hopping over here to get something to eat!
>
> Dionne (*screams of excitement*): He's coming to say hi to us!
>
> Holly: Is he going to eat the grass? He is! He's nibbling on the grass! (*Holly can hardly stand still, she is so excited.*)
>
> Charlie: We're so lucky! (*He sighs contentedly.*) A bunny!
>
> More children rush to the window to see the rabbit. It continues to eat the spring grass, then hops off out of the school yard.

A simple experience such as this one can often fuel children's excitement and enthusiasm about animals for days, even weeks with the right support. When children are visited by an animal, such as a ladybug that crawls onto a child's arm or a rabbit that hops through the school yard, children do indeed feel lucky. It's as if they've been given a pass into the world of animals—and for a moment they get to glimpse inside. As I wrote in chapter 3, children explore issues of power and vulnerability when they interact with animals. Encountering a "wild" animal in real life is no different. They feel lucky and special to have encountered an animal who, of its own accord, has come to pay them a visit.

Bringing a child to a wild place, a wooded park, or even just a backyard where there are opportunities to encounter wildlife can be a life-changing experience for a child. In many cases, those unique moments of encountering wild animals ignite a spark of curiosity and wonder about wild animals and their place in the world. When children are indulged and supported in their love and reverence for animals, that love expands and is generalized to other living creatures and the environment. And what better place to do that than in nature, the home of animals? When children are allowed opportunities to be awed by animals, they grow in many ways. A natural setting is a place not created by adults, and it's a place with its own rules. Being a part of this world is special and meaningful for young children and adults alike. Experiences in nature that are specifically focused on animals or searching for animals can support children's development in these areas as well. Chapter 5 has some examples for wildlife games and nature search activities that support children's innate love for wild places and the animals who live there.

Clearly, there is no shortage of animals in children's lives. We feed our children many ideas and perceptions of animals. It's important that we, as parents and educators, consider what our portrayals of animals really are. Children have such an attraction to animals: all the information they get from animals, whether they are family or classroom pets, wild animals, zoo animals, toys, media, or other products, affects their understanding of animals. We need to look at the overt and the covert things we are telling children about animals so that we can pass on the messages we really mean.

Creating Authentic Experiences with Animals

A first-grade class has been curious about birds. Linda, their teacher, helped them create a bird feeding area outside the classroom window. They purchased feeders, and some parents donated birdseed to the class. The children store a clipboard and pencil on a shelf near the window, along with some easy-to-use binoculars, and keep a running list of the birds that visit the feeders. When they aren't sure of the species, they check their bird identification guides. They are learning to identify birds by color, shape, size, and even behavior.

Some of the children make observational drawings of the chickadees that visit the feeder. They mix paint colors to find just the right shades of gray to color their birds. Other children are researching the migratory path of other species they have seen at the feeders and are creating a map that shows the route the birds take to their wintering grounds. Still others have been doing a project to compare which birdseed mixes attract the most species of birds. There is a reading area with fiction and nonfiction books about birds, and there are comfortable chairs and cushions near the windows for the children to sit on while they read or simply relax and watch the birds.

You've likely been thinking a great deal about how your program offers children experiences with animals. You may be considering classroom pets, but for whatever reason, you aren't yet ready. Perhaps you want to approach animal-based field trips in different ways. Maybe you're interested in some meaningful long-term projects to introduce and develop with your class or your own children. Maybe you're still mulling over the many ways that you can create animal connections for children. The good news is that there are easy, thoughtful ways to bring children and animals together. Through scientific inquiry, intentionally planned field trips, and opportunities for creative expression, you can provide ways for children to think about animals that will help them develop empathy, compassion, and an awareness of species other than themselves.

This chapter looks at the many different ways you can help children form strong, meaningful bonds with animals—what I call "authentic experiences." Through authentic animal experiences, children are developing certain thinking skills and deepening their knowledge across the scope of disciplines: language and literacy, the arts, science, math, even social studies. Following this chapter, chapter 6 explores the dimensions of bringing animals into the classroom. But whether or not you choose to host an animal in your classroom, you can help children develop special relationships with animals in a variety of ways.

Throughout this book, and in this chapter especially, I use the term *authentic experiences* to refer to experiences that portray animals in ways that are as genuine and realistic as possible. Authentic materials—say, a picture of a real dog as opposed to a picture of a cartoon dog—offer children a sense of an animal's actual size, shape, color, and texture. They may hint at the animal's behavior or habitat. Authentic experiences, such as observing actual insects, which eat, move, and pupate, engage children in using their hands and all of their senses, in ways that passive experiences, such as worksheets, lectures, demonstrations, or even a plastic "life cycle set" of insect replicas, cannot.

The activity ideas in this chapter are springboards for you to use to think about bringing authentic experiences to children. The chapter outlines several approaches, some more scientifically or creatively focused, to bringing animals into children's lives. As your authentic animal experiences develop with the children's interests, you may explore animals in ways that are brand new to you, too! The ideas in this chapter will help children do the following:

- practice scientific inquiry, through involving them in developmentally appropriate research that strengthens their observation, analysis, and questioning skills and gives them practice synthesizing information and drawing conclusions

- learn math skills, through counting and grouping animals, measuring them, and creating structures for them

- practice language and literacy, through reading, writing, and storytelling

DOMESTIC CAT

More	Middle	Less
Children read nonfiction books about cats and look at posters and other real images. Their prior knowledge, questions, and observations about cats are assessed through conversation and class discussions. Children's words are noted on a class chart for reference. Teacher arranges to have a real cat visit the classroom.	An "exploration station" has plastic or wooden "realistic" replicas of cats. Life-size stuffed animals are brought in for children to compare and contrast.	Posters depicting cartoon images hang around the room. Children are given plastic toy cats that wear clothing, live in houses, and drive cars. Teacher provides coloring sheets of cats. Little if any discussion about cats occurs.

MONARCH CATERPILLAR

More	Middle	Less
Teacher responsibly obtains real caterpillars, which are then properly housed, reared, and allowed to pupate in classroom. Children read nonfiction books about monarch caterpillars and watch time-lapse videos of their life cycle. Class conducts research on monarch migration and releases butterflies.	Pinned/mounted butterfly specimens of species not native to the school's geographic locale are provided, as are plastic replicas of eggs, caterpillars, pupa, and moths/butterflies.	Children make macaroni "diagram" of caterpillar life cycle. Teacher posts pictures of cartoon butterflies with four legs, toothy grins, and pilot's goggles.

ELEPHANT

More	Middle	Less
Teacher plans a field trip to a local zoo. She prepares and assesses children's understanding and feelings about elephants. The children identify ideas and questions they have about elephants and conduct age-appropriate research about elephants in the wild using nonfiction books and documentary videos about elephants.	Teacher plans a field trip to a local zoo. Before the field trip, the children read children's literature with cartoon elephants that behave like elephants. Children visit the zoo, and when they return, they move onto a new "science unit."	No field trip is planned; instead the children play with toy elephants and read stories about elephants doing human things. They create art projects out of paper plates painted gray with strips of gray flannel glued to the center for "trunks."

- express their feelings and observations about animals through creative expressions like painting, sketching, and dramatic play

- explore and reflect on their own understanding about social connections and the relationship between humans and animals

Engaging the hearts of young children should be first and foremost in any exploration or encounters with animals. After all, it's through the heart that most of us made our first connections with animals, and those initial feelings of curiosity, love, and excitement are what made many of you animal lovers to this day. This is by far the most effective way to help children form strong, lasting bonds with animals.

AUTHENTIC EXPERIENCES THROUGH INQUIRY-BASED LEARNING

Inquiry-based learning builds upon a child's actual experience and inspires questions to help children "construct" learning based on information they already know. Ideally, inquiry should be thought of as a process and a set of skills that children—and scientists alike—use to find out more about the world. Important scientific thinking skills, such as observing, asking questions, making predictions, describing, and drawing conclusions, are all practices of scientific inquiry.

Educators can look for opportunities to engage children in scientific inquiry—they are everywhere! For example, a child who has grown up in a northern climate will be familiar with snow and cold weather. Her experience with freezing temperatures, sleet, and snowfall will form the first piece of her bigger picture of weather and the effect of temperature changes on the environment. An important element of inquiry happens when the child identifies what she knows and asks questions based on what she has experienced: *I feel the temperature getting colder, and I wonder what will happen to the pond when the water freezes. What will the ducks and fish do?*

An adult can support the child's learning through inquiry by helping the child articulate her observations and then formulate questions based on what she is observing (or not observing, in some cases). Together, they might create experiments and investigate further, or the adult may help the child conduct other research when appropriate. For older children this might include taking water samples and measuring the temperature of the water, reading books, and watching documentaries about nature in winter. Inquiry will include asking many questions throughout the process of discovery, making observations (for example, watching the ducks, looking for the fish each day), making predictions (such as whether or when ice will form), recording data (such as the temperature or the behavior of the animals, perhaps in a daily log of findings), and most importantly, trying things out firsthand (touching the water and talking about its temperature).

In early childhood, scientific inquiry involves encouraging children to test their own ideas and questions through exploration and experimentation. Scientific inquiry builds knowledge based on the results of those explorations. Children naturally work to understand things through repeated experiences with different materials and conditions. Their exploration leads to further observations and predictions. Educators and parents can help children build their understanding by asking them to make observations about what they know and to make predictions about what will happen based on their past experience.

Inquiry-based learning also demands that educators be responsive to children's interests, motivations, and questions as well as their emerging ideas and explanations. In supporting scientific inquiry, it's important to remember that even those ideas and explanations that aren't "correct" have immense value. They are important pieces of children's growing awareness and understanding of the world around them and the way things work. Teachers or parents who wish to include more inquiry-based experiences in their programs should pay close attention to the natural curiosities that emerge as children play and interact with one another.

A class of curious four-year-olds goes outdoors to play each afternoon just before lunch. They notice the snow melting little by little each day, the green of the grass getting bolder and bolder, the trees leafing out, and eventually dandelions popping up in the school yard. Noting their observations, the teacher helps them craft questions: *Why does this part of the yard have more dandelions than this part? Why is there still snow under the slide when there is none left anywhere else on the playground? Could we find more spots where there is still snow? Spots where there are dandelions? What do those places have in common? How are they different from one another?*

In this setting, a teacher supports inquiry by creating lots of opportunities for the children to be outside as the seasons change. He asks the children questions and listens closely to their responses, helping himself and the children understand their observations about the seasonal changes they see occurring. He listens to their words, teases out their questions, and crafts experiences based on these things. He creates experiences designed to generate children's ideas about what they see and observe and what they want to learn. For example, the teacher might create many opportunities for children to explore the playground, then encourage them to notice and describe what they see. He might challenge the children to think about different ways to measure the temperatures or other ways to note similarities and differences in different areas of the school yard.

The teacher could help older children recognize the temperature variations, then provide them with thermometers to measure the different temperatures throughout the school yard and at different times during the day. This might lead to observations about seasonal changes other than temperature. Children might start observing and discussing the animal species they see or hear around the school yard as the seasons change, an activity that might lead into explorations of which animals hibernate. For younger children, this inquiry may lead to other questions about where animals go as the seasons change, what they do in response to the colder temperatures, and what they do as the temperatures begin to climb in early spring.

Children might also notice a distinct lack of insect visitors around the school yard, and this might lead to an investigation about what happens to insects when the weather turns cold and what happens as the weather warms. Since the children have experienced these seasonal changes already, they are naturally more aware of subtle changes that happen as the weather warms. Because the class's explorations grow from the group's questions and are responses to the very things the children expressed interest in, the children are more invested in the experiences than might have been otherwise. And finally, since each facet of this exploration is experienced firsthand, with the children fully engaged in their surroundings and free to make their own observations, the learning that takes place is more concrete and relevant than it would be if taught, through, say, cut-and-paste charts about plant life cycles or animal migration patterns.

While the value of inquiry is more in the process of discovery and exploration than it is in the "correct answer," it is important that educators have enough knowledge about the topics at hand to introduce concepts and support children's investigations.

An Example of the Inquiry Spectrum: Exploring Birds

Parents and teachers can help support authentic animal experiences through inquiry. Scientific inquiry is a spectrum, stretching from very unstructured, "open-ended" inquiry experiences to more guided, directed inquiry experiences. Neither approach is better than the other, and each type of exploration can help children learn about different aspects of an animal. When children are first introduced to materials or a topic, very open-ended experiences allow them lots of latitude to "go where they will" and follow their questions and observations. Then, as they gain more familiarity and experience with the topic, they will focus more closely and, with an adult's help, might be guided into more structured exploration.

For example, if a teacher wants to support her students' interest in birds, there are several ways she could approach the topic through inquiry.

A teacher, Miss Brittany, wants to support inquiry. She might be aware that for some time the children in her class have been noticing birds, watching them through the window and talking about the birds they've seen in their yards or on nature walks. The children describe and imitate how birds move and eat and the noises birds make. To create more opportunities for the children to see and learn about real birds, Miss Brittany helps them make and put up birdfeeders outside the classroom window so they can watch birds more frequently. The children notice some birds on the feeders and some that always eat from the ground. Their observations lead to many questions: *Why is that? Maybe the birds on the ground are too heavy for the feeder? Maybe they like different kinds of food? What if we try putting out different types of food to see if different birds like different foods?*

Miss Brittany further supports their exploration by providing binoculars, clipboards, papers, paint, and markers. Excited about the new materials they have available, the children begin to draw some of the birds they see. Many of them are especially interested in sizes, shapes, and colors of the birds and pay particular attention to these elements in their drawings and paintings.

Miss Brittany supports the children through questioning. By asking them to describe their drawings and explain their notes and by listening carefully to their discussions, questions, and ideas about birds, she can gauge their understanding. Sharing observations and ideas is an important scientific thinking skill. It is a key element in inquiry.

In the meantime, the class is also putting out different types of food for the birds and collecting data about how much of each type gets eaten. The children make charts, draw pictures, and even observe the amount of bird food consumed each day (by watching the level of food in the feeders get lower and lower). Together, they generate some ideas about different birds' favorite foods. In their observing, they've also begun to notice and talk about the birds' body parts and what parts birds use to get their food and to move around. New attention is focused on beaks, legs, feathers, and wings as the children watch the birds as they move, eating and hopping around the feeding station.

Miss Brittany provides the children with a variety of books, including field guides, photography books, and other books featuring images of the different birds the children have observed firsthand. These books allow the children opportunities to see the birds and their body parts more closely. In this example, the teacher's role became more pronounced and more directive as the children's investigations became more focused.

Open-ended inquiry experiences work well in environments where children and adults are comfortable with looser structure, (usually) lots of noise, and a great deal of movement and hands-on exploration. Often, the more open inquiry activities allow a class to arrive at many different conclusions. For example, in the experience described above, some children will be more focused and engaged in explorations about coloration and patterns in birds, while others will be more interested in discovering how birds move the way they do. Still others will be intensely curious about which birds prefer which types of seed and how their beaks help them eat.

To support the children's learning, an educator will "stand back" as much as possible, noting children's reactions, jotting down their questions, and guiding them toward (in this case) a deeper understanding of birds, beaks, feathers, and other topics. The teacher directs the inquiry, though not necessarily its outcome, by asking the children for more information about their observations and helping them determine ways to find answers. The teacher supports inquiry in many different ways and plays a larger role as investigations become more structured over time.

Very open inquiry experiences may better suit children who are a bit older, more adept at synthesizing information and experiences, and more comfortable with their own autonomy. A more "teacher-guided" inquiry experience will encourage children to use specific materials or tools to answer a question posed by the teacher. A teacher may have formulated specific ideas she hopes the children will investigate, such as, using the bird example above, the idea that different feathers have different functions. The teacher could provide tools, such as magnifying lenses, photos of birds and birds in flight, and an assortment of feathers, to help the children learn about the form and function of feathers. The teacher might demonstrate how to use specific tools or ask specific questions to help the children focus on a particular aspect of the feathers.

The term *teacher-guided inquiry* refers to science explorations that are largely driven by the teacher or guide. The more structure an educator provides for an experience, the less "open" the inquiry. However, structure can also help children narrow their questions and investigations, allowing for creativity within the parameters. Children are still quite free to experiment, ask questions, and "play" with materials, within a context that the teacher has provided.

Using inquiry-based lessons to create authentic animal experiences is a natural fit. Seeing a variety of real animals and having authentic experiences with animals, observing their behavior firsthand, is extremely important for these investigations. The example bird activity given above can extend many days or weeks in the classroom at many levels of "open" or "directed" inquiry.

As you begin to talk about and explore animals more fully, you can use the opportunity to gauge the children's understanding. What do they already know about animals? Intentional listening and documenting can help you determine children's baseline level of knowledge about a certain topic. It can also help children clarify their understanding. Listening to children is a form of "preassessment." As your studies progress, continue these group discussions and note how the group is expanding their knowledge base about different topics and deepening their understanding. Chances are, your own knowledge and understanding of the subject will increase as well. "Circling back," or revisiting a topic later on, as children's interests change is another way to deepen everyone's learning. They will make new and different connections each time a topic is visited. If the class is interested in food and nutrition, for example, you might recall the experiences you had with birds' beaks and the different foods that birds need to survive and thrive.

It's not within the scope of this book to explain scientific inquiry in great detail, but several resources are readily available. I suggest any educator or parent interested in scientific inquiry seek out resources that specifically address the learning needs of young children and that approach STEM (science, technology, engineering, and mathematics) education in a developmentally appropriate way. Redleaf Press, the National Association for the

Education of Young Children, and the National Science Teachers Association all offer lots of resources to support those working with young children who want to provide exciting, meaningful science experiences (see appendix A, Additional Resources, for links to these organizations). Suffice it to say that inquiry is scientific exploration based on questioning and curiosity and that you don't have to know all the answers. Your role as an educator is to support children's questions and explorations by providing them with tools and opportunities to learn more, as well as to prepare yourself ahead of time by developing and deepening your own knowledge in the topics you explore with your students. Above all, be responsive to their questions, welcome their ideas, and support their learning through providing lots of authentic, real-world opportunities and experiences with animals.

Another Example of Inquiry: Researching Frogs

Another way to introduce authentic animal inquiry is to ask children about their interests. If children in the classroom are particularly interested in one species of animal, asking them, "What are you wondering about?" can be a great jumping-off point for a class-wide research project. Suppose the class is interested in frogs. You can explore this topic together in a number of ways:

- Encourage everyone in the class to bring from home one or two representations of a frog. These might be pictures from books, stuffed frogs, toy frogs, or photographs. Although you may already have many of these things in the classroom, inviting the children to bring something from home builds investment in the activity and also serves to pique curiosity: *I wonder why we're bringing these things?*

- Be sure to include some scientifically accurate photos of real frogs in their real habitats. Visit your library for nonfiction books about frogs.

- If you have the means, find some Internet videos or clips of frog sounds so that children can hear the animals and see them moving in real life. Set aside an area in the classroom for frog-related objects. Use the collection as a springboard for discussion.

- Allow plenty of time for children to share what they know about frogs. Create a list together. Some of the questions you might discuss: *Do all of these frogs look alike? How are they different? What do they all have in common?* Talk about the characteristics of each image or representation. Be sure to compare them to images of real frogs so the children can make distinctions between artistic or playful representations and realistic portrayals. Jot down the words children use when describing frogs.

- Encourage older children to practice writing their words themselves. In doing this exercise, I've heard children use words such as "slimy," "greenish with spots," "big eyes," and "wet skin." Encourage all contributions. Invite children to elaborate on what they mean, providing as much detail as they can. Encourage them to notice and describe similarities and differences. Do all frogs have the same pattern? Find out together. Ask them to make observations using other senses. For example, if all the observations are based on visual cues, ask the children about it: *Has anyone ever heard a frog before? If so, what did it sound like? Has anyone ever felt a frog? What did it feel like?*

- If some of the portrayals show the frog in a particular setting (such as a pond, lake, car, school), discuss what it looks like to see a frog in that setting. Does it seem funny or strange? Is this a place you would expect to see frogs? Where might we find frogs in real life? Would we ever expect to see a frog in a school? Under what circumstances? Look through the images, and talk about what you can observe about how frogs might move. For example, do they all have four legs? Describe a frog's body. Do any of the frogs have flippers? Do the frogs have clothes on? Why or why not?

- Ask the children how they could categorize the images or figures. Some examples may be "real" or "not real," "happy" or "sad," "in nature" or "not in nature." They might use a variety of words to describe their categories, based on emotions, physical characteristics, context, behavior, and so on.

- Use the children's words and observations to make a "KWL" chart—what we *know*, what we *want to know*, and finally, later, what we *learned*. This chart is helpful because it shows the children their ideas are worth documenting. It is also a convenient "parking spot" for questions that the children have and serves to remind you what questions remain for later exploration and discovery.

- Compile a list of the children's questions, and begin informal research together to discover the answers. Perhaps these questions will inspire a visit to a local nature center or park. You might contact your county extension office and invite an educator to come in to speak with the class.

These are explorations that should happen often, because as children's knowledge grows, so will their questions. These questions can lead to rich discussions about animals. Animals are portrayed in so many different ways, and this activity will make that very clear! The point of this exercise is not to pass judgment on one book or toy or photo versus another, it is simply to compare and note differences and similarities. You can use these discussions as a springboard for more scientific inquiry.

Inquiry through Place-Based Education

Inquiry through place-based learning is one of the most authentic ways that educators can bring animal experiences into the curriculum. Place-based education uses local or regional phenomena, conditions, events, and organisms as a context or tool with which to teach curriculum. Place-based education is helpful in engaging students of all ages because it occurs right where the children live. It's accessible: often teachers can simply take a class outdoors to learn. Even in the most urbanized areas, place-based educational opportunities abound. Research supports the value of involving children in hands-on experiences in their own communities. And time in nature can help children sharpen their senses: listening for birdsong, squirrel chatter, or the buzzing of cicadas on a warm summer afternoon can be a delightful opportunity to help children develop their physical senses. Place-based education can be done any time, anywhere:

- Take your class outdoors to look for living creatures and compare them to nonliving creatures to further children's understanding of the difference between living and nonliving organisms (a first-grade science standard). Taking the children outside regularly to look for animals or animal signs can extend the lesson into a phenology (study of seasonal changes) experience as well. Because the learning takes place in the children's own backyards and centers on animals they know and are familiar with, the curriculum is more meaningful, their connections with those animals stronger.

- Learn about animals that are indigenous (local) to your area. Children can learn about an animal's habitat, feeding habits, behavior, and life cycle. If your school has a natural area that might support a particular species of animal, go outdoors and search for signs the animal has been there. Bring in maps to look at together, identifying the animal's home range.

- Take frequent nature walks with your child or class. Even if you don't have access to an expansive natural area, you can explore your immediate surroundings for signs of wildlife. A rapidly growing body of research affirms the notion that children's development is influenced positively by frequent hands-on experiences in the natural world. Nature speaks to a child's aesthetic sensibility—his sense of form, color, texture, and beauty. Use opportunities to look at birds and other wild animals: notice their shapes and colors. How are they alike? How are they different? How many different colors can children identify? Challenging children to find insects of many different colors, or to describe the pattern or behavior of a bird supports language and literacy and sharpens observation skills.

- Look for evidence of animal activity, such as tracks, scats (animal droppings), and nests in the trees (winter is an especially good time to look for unused nests, depending on the climate in your area, because the lack of leaves on the trees helps children find nests). Walk through a forest, and try to find animal trails through the leaves or matted-down grass where animals like deer may have slept. Search for toads and turtles burrowed under the leaves. Turn over logs and rocks in search of invertebrates like pill bugs, millipedes, and beetles. Playing in nature gives children opportunities to develop cognitive skills like problem solving.

- Sprinkle a little sugar on the sidewalk, and you will have the opportunity to watch ants for a long time. This can be fascinating and quite exciting for young children. Speculate as a group where the ants are going, what they're doing, and how they found the sugar. The important thing is that you allow children the opportunity to watch, talk about what they are seeing, and feel their sense of reverence for these animals in the wild that are behaving of their own accord in their own world.

- Locate an "adopt an animal" program at a zoo or nature center through which donations help support an animal through care products, food, and other supplies. For example, a group of schoolchildren "adopted" a native snake that was an exhibit animal at a local nature center. The children sold their own artwork to raise funds for "Liz" the snake. The money went directly to the nature center, where staff purchased supplies and materials necessary for Liz's care and well-being. The project involved having the children research Liz's needs and how they could meet them. A naturalist brought Liz to the classroom for an educational visit. These nature experiences are worthwhile in their own right, but they become intentionally place-based lessons when you help children recognize the different ecosystems the animals depend on, how they are unique to that child's own home range, and where in a child's immediate world these animals might be found. A class could explore the natural environment in the school yard and neighborhood to learn what species might have lived there (or still do!).

Inquiry-based research explores a wide variety of topics. Although it may seem like a simple exploration of representations of one kind of animal, it's actually helping children develop many important skills. In exploring their observations and questions about animals, children are learning about the following:

- an animal's body and special physical adaptations

- an animal's real-life behavior and behavioral adaptations

- an animal's habitat and possibly other animals that share the same habitat

- different ways of portraying and representing animals

- the difference between realistic and "not-realistic" portrayals

There are many different approaches to inquiry, and the way you choose to focus your inquiry will depend on the children and their contributions and observations. The act of discussing and comparing will help children think more deeply about whatever animal your activity centers around. An inquiry-based approach also helps children formulate and articulate their own questions and direct their own learning. All of these contribute to a more authentic experience of the animal world.

AUTHENTIC EXPERIENCES THROUGH FIELD TRIPS

Field trips to zoos, aquariums, and nature centers often are the highlight of the school year for both children and adults. These experiences can be an important stepping-stone in children's learning and development with animals. Education and conservation-oriented organizations are beginning to recognize the importance of providing young children with authentic, meaningful experiences and in many cases are changing the way they offer those experiences to better deliver what young children need.

Planning an Authentic Field Trip Experience

Field trips to zoos, museums, and aquariums provide children with real-life experiences with animals and can be meaningful and memorable for even very young children. However, many field trips happen with little planning or forethought on the part of the teacher. These visits are exciting, to be sure, but in many cases they are mere cursory introductions to a topic, a place, or a group of animals. Once the group returns to the classroom, little if any work may be done to reinforce the children's learning, ignite the sparks of curiosity, or satisfy the questions that undoubtedly arise. The visit is simply over, and the group moves on to other topics and themes.

On the other hand, with some preparation and consideration, educators can ensure that the children make deeper connections with the animals they encounter. David Sobel, a renowned environmental educator, states that children need to have an intimate knowledge of familiar animals before they can be expected to care for more "abstract" animals that they are less likely to encounter. Here are ideas for ways to thoughtfully introduce animals to children:

- Before deciding to take a class field trip, you may want to do a bit of research. Deciding where to take your class can take time, but it is well worth it. Consider your class's interest. What has the group been working on or become curious about? Insects? Perhaps a child has recently been on vacation to the ocean, and this sparked a whole class interest in marine mammals. What season is it? Are there birds migrating or animals preparing to hibernate? Are certain species of animals especially intriguing to your group? Maybe a favorite class story features a certain species of animal. Can you take the class to see a live animal of the same species?

- Learn about the resources available to you locally. Are there places that could provide special experiences for your group? For example, many small nature centers offer naturalist tours or programs at little to no cost for school groups. If you tell them of a specific interest or animal you are studying, they may be able to offer you special resources, such as bones, furs, eggs, or feathers. They may offer to take your class on a hike to see that animal's habitat and to provide activities related to that animal. On the other hand, bigger operations, such as zoos, will likely have more of a one-size-fits-all approach but will be able to offer the children a much bigger collection of animals.

- Once you've decided on your location, consider what your group will do while there. Will you hike? Observe animals in exhibits? Will a naturalist or other educator lead your group in an activity? Will the children be able to ask questions? How will you ensure that the children have time to explore on their own, formulating questions and ideas they can bring back to the classroom? What are your teaching outcomes for the visit? Do you want to simply introduce an animal, group of animals, or habitats, allowing children time to digest the information and get "primed" for classroom activities you'll do later? Or do you have specific educational goals for the visit, such as learning to identify groups of animals or learning the names of certain species of birds? Whatever your outcome, be clear about your group's needs. Talk ahead of time, if possible, with the staff so they can be sure to help you reach your stated objectives for the visit. Many nature centers, zoos, and wildlife refuges offer information packets to help teachers prepare for visits. Often a quick visit to a site's website will yield more ideas for educators as well.

- You may wish to create KWL charts before field trips. KWL charts— what we *know*, what we *want to know*, and later, what we *learned*—can be created by a group of children together with a teacher. This helps to establish a baseline of what the children understand and know about the animals you'll be visiting. Perhaps you'll be visiting a bird sanctuary on the coast. Ask them what the habitat is that you'll be visiting together. Ask the children what they know about the species of animals that live there and why that habitat is important. Invite them to tell you everything they know about your destination, and then, in the spirit of inquiry, move into the "W" section—what do you want to know? Identifying questions ahead of time helps children to search for meaning in the experience, and it also builds investment in the visit. If five-year-old McKenzie is curious "why pelicans have a big pouch under their beaks," you can bet she is going to spend at least some of her time at the bird sanctuary thinking about that.

- Allow children enough time to explore freely during the field trip. Children will naturally be curious about a new place, and everyone's chances for a successful visit increase if you include time for them to indulge this curiosity. Plan time for them to wander around the nature center, look at exhibits, and run around outside if there's an appropriate place to do so. They will be excited and eager to explore. The specialness of the field trip starts before you even leave the classroom, so remember to indulge their excitement when you can. Remember that in many cases field trips are that much more special because they are experiences children share with special friends or close family members.

- Take plenty of pictures, and document the children's words on the field trip if you can. Give the children time to document their own feelings, words, and observations. Write down the questions they have and the feelings they express. Later you can use their journals or sketches as well as your photos and words to jog memories and spark discussions about the field trip and what you did.

- Be sure to ask a naturalist or guide if you may collect natural objects, such as seedpods, sand, grasses, or other treasures the children find while you're there. If so, plan to bring the treasures back to the classroom for later use.

- Once you return to the classroom, review what your group did and discovered. If you have a morning meeting, you may wish to start the day by asking the children to share their favorite memory of the day or tell one thing they remember about the trip. Again, allow plenty of time for this discussion. As a group, you might also create a list of words related to your field trip. The words you choose should be designed to spark thinking. Write them on strips of paper, and place them in a hat. Have a child draw one word out of the hat—for example, *salamander*—and ask the children to tell you some things they know about salamanders.

If you choose a destination because it supports a project or unit your class is already working on, you will find many ways to integrate what you've learned into your classroom activities. See more ways to explore in the sections on literacy, language, and dramatic arts.

Bringing the Zoo Home: Supporting the Field Trip Experience

Children's learning experiences can also be extended beyond the field trip. An example of a great hands-on experience for children is the special zoo just for young children at the Brookfield Zoo, near Chicago. There you will find many tools to engage children in caring for animals. For example, there is a "veterinary clinic" complete with real medical equipment, stainless steel tables (which are the perfect height for children), clipboards for taking notes on the animals' conditions, and assorted stuffed animals in crates, ready to be cared for. Children can don lab coats and set to work examining different animals. Children perform "checkups" with real stethoscopes, otoscopes, scales, and blood pressure monitors. "Injured" stuffed animals may need the children to administer bandages or wrap broken bones.

For children who want to participate in care for real animals, many exciting opportunities await them in the "household pets zoo." Here, children can help feed or brush common pets such as cats, guinea pigs, hamsters, and reptiles, animals they are likely somewhat familiar with. By focusing on animals that are already familiar to most children, the zoo helps children develop strong bonds and connections with these animals. As they grow, children who have had these authentic interactions expand their sense of

love and stewardship for animals, and they go on to develop strong bonds with other, more "exotic" animals. In the household pets section, children open up, ask questions, and engage in dialogue with the others there. Educators and parents can build on children's existing comfort with animals by simply offering them opportunities to share their own stories about familiar animals.

This children's zoo is a great example of an authentic experience children can have caring for, relating to, and playing with animals without going on "exotic" field trips. How can educators or parents replicate such experiences in the classroom or at home? Here are some ideas:

- Provide real medical equipment such as gauze bandages, stethoscopes, scales, and more. The more genuine, the better. Encourage the children to give animals a checkup and ask them lots of questions about the pet's health. Perhaps you can be the client, bringing a stuffed pet with the chicken pox for little vets-in-training to examine. You need do little more than jump in and play with the children on their terms.

- Offer children plenty of opportunities to share stories with you and other interested adults about their own pets, the pets they know, and other familiar animals. Children need to know that adults value their thoughts, feelings, and words. Show them that they matter by listening attentively and engaging in dialogue with them about animals.

- Provide children with ways of connecting with animals that respond to children's unique learning styles. Create classroom areas for children to be quiet and pensive, or areas where children can be loud and animated. Children can play at caregiving in a veterinary area with stuffed animals, real medical equipment, and more. Create an "animal shelter" where children can groom and care for stuffed animals. Or work together to set up a "zoo" where children can guide others on tours and teach them about animals. Often all that's required are some cuddly stuffed animals (which the children would probably love to bring from home!), boxes for the "kennels," and perhaps brushes, bandages, or other equipment. Check around your home or center to see what you have that you could make available. Hit some garage sales to obtain real animal tools such as pet dishes, brushes, leashes, and more. Enlist the children in creating kennels or houses for the animals out of boxes.

- Build time into your schedule for free, dramatic play. Let children dress and act like certain animals, and give them materials to create their own costumes and representations. It may take a few weeks for children (especially older children) to recognize opportunities for imaginary play. We know that allowing them the freedom to "become" animals can be a powerful way to support children's developing empathy and love for animals. When they "become" animals, children look at the world through that animal's eyes. Offer children many opportunities to play at caregiving and connecting with imaginary and real animals. Setting up dramatic animal play areas in your classroom or home is another powerful way to help children develop empathy and love for animals through caregiving and pretend play. Both kinds of experiences can be authentic and influential for children.

Field trips can be special and meaningful experiences. Or they can be chaotic and hectic and can try your patience. Through careful preparation and planning, you can offer field trip experiences that are really enjoyable and memorable for children. By keeping in mind your educational goals to offer special and authentic experiences between children and animals, you can create great field trips.

AUTHENTIC EXPERIENCES
THROUGH CREATIVE EXPRESSION

Literacy

Animals often provide the perfect motivation to help children share stories, feelings, ideas, and more. Educators can use children's natural attraction to animals to help inspire art and literacy activities. Since children love to talk about, read about, and ask questions about animals, there is no limit to the number of ways that animals can help children gain skills and practice in language, literacy, and arts.

- Make "animal stories" a part of your routine in the classroom. Every child has at least one favorite story to tell about an animal. Invite each child to bring in a photo of their pet or a pet they wish they had, and share about that animal. Encouraging them to share their words and experiences with real animals will deepen their connections to those animals. It also builds on literacy and language learning by engaging them in dialogue with their peers and inspiring them to articulate their feelings. For a longer-term project, invite them to write stories in an "animal journal" that chronicles the life and adventures of their own pets, their friends' pets, or other familiar animals, such as backyard birds or squirrels. There are many ways you can approach this. Make talking about the animals a normal part of every day. Ask the children questions about the images and animals. Even if they can't yet answer you clearly, they will most certainly be thinking and making connections.

- Encourage children to write about different animal species. They might make up fantasy stories and write them down, or dictate to you or another adult, who can record their words on pages to accompany pictures the children draw. For an experience like this to really build connections with animals and deepen children's understandings, plan to really take your time. Start by brainstorming a list of animals together. This list can be built for days leading up to the start of the activity, as children will add to it, be inspired by the shared time brainstorming, and get new ideas at home, too.

- Invite children to choose a favorite animal. Offer plenty of pictures, books, and other images that children can look at to pique their curiosity about animals. Invite each child to spend as much time as he needs considering which animal to choose for this project. Once each child has chosen an animal, create a list and post it prominently for the whole class to see.

- Encourage the children to immerse themselves in research. Depending on the ages of the children, this research might be simply looking at pictures online or at the local library, or perhaps visiting a library and checking out materials that the children can take home. Other examples of research are conducting personal interviews with family or friends, and watching the actual animal in a setting the child can visit. Invite them to think also about aspects such as the animal's habitat needs, food, and where in the world it might be found. Help the children combine everything they have learned into posters, scrapbooks, or other displays to be shared with the class. They may enjoy "presenting their research" to one another.

- In determining where a favorite animal lives, go beyond simply "the zoo." If a child chooses an animal that doesn't live in your region, say, a zebra, research and find out together where zebras really live. Perhaps

post a large world map, and help the children locate the regions in which their animal is found. Invite the children to write or draw a story about the place you researched, or an animal that lives there.

- Create a book about animals. Have each child draw one page in the book. Encourage individual expression, since children may wish to create realistic drawings or fantasy drawings. Under their picture, the children can label their animal and write one or two things they love about it. You can make color copies, bind the pages together with ribbon or twine, and provide one book to each child. A project like this can also build community in the classroom, providing rich material for discussion and opportunities for children to share stories. Children love to talk about their favorite animals with each other, and creating a book together helps children share responsibility and pride in creating something as a group that will be a shared treasure.

One classroom teacher invited children to create a book about their favorite animals. The book was part of a larger classroom exploration of compassion and what it means to be kind and humane. In addition to having the children articulate what they liked about animals, the teacher wanted to encourage the children to think about hope and gratitude. The teacher asked the students to think about what they were thankful for and what their dreams were. They drew animals and completed either of the sentences, "I am thankful for ___" or "I have a dream that ___." The teacher said that in addition to helping children with literacy and language skills, creating a book offered this class a creative opportunity "to put their own ideas into action to care for animals, protect their habitats, and promote compassion, empathy, coexistence, and peace."

- If you've collected natural materials on a field trip, invite the class to make a group collage, or allow the children to work individually on dimensional projects related to the site or the animals that live there. Consider printing your photos from the day and having the children give you the captions. Create a large class poster or photo book about the field trip.

Projects that involve the group can be a wonderful way for children to share their loving feelings about animals with one another. They can also help demystify feelings the other children may have. For example, if a child is particularly fond of snakes and the other children don't like them, she can be an ambassador who teaches other children all the great things she knows about snakes!

Language and Thinking about Animals

Class discussions about animals are another way to provide authentic experiences with animals while supporting children's literacy and language development. Encourage group discussions about animals and the different words and language we use to talk about animals. As explored in chapter 4, the labels we group animals under can be an interesting topic for discussion. If you know that the children understand the meaning of the word "category," you can start a classroom discussion there. Even very young children will be curious about these distinctions and will be able to participate in the discussion. As I did in chapter 4, I want to stress that the point of having conversations about these categories is not to change anyone's mind about anything or to make value judgments about someone's individual or cultural attitudes about a particular species. The purpose of these discussions is simply one of exploration. Awareness of the ways in which we relate to different animals is one step in deepening those relationships. Here are some ways to explore language:

- Ask the children to place certain animals in groups, and then invite them to explain to you what those groups are and why they were selected. To make the discussion more concrete, use photos, realistic-looking toys or replicas, or accurate illustrations of animals to aid the children's comprehension. This can be a meaningful class activity. Be sure to note the words and explanations each child uses when describing their reasoning about placing animals in certain categories. Ask children to clarify their thinking with questions such as, "Could that animal fit into another category? Which one?" and "Do you think a farm animal could be a pet?"

- Allow time for respectful discussion and for children to learn from one another's conclusions and observations about animals. Encourage children to share their personal experiences and think critically about how they decided to put animals into one category or another. Ask them, "Why do you think we group animals into categories?" If possible, refrain from sharing your own views, as many children will follow an adult's lead when it comes to feelings about animals. This exercise is intended to help children recognize the categories and to help them learn about the ways in which our culture views animals.

- Foster respectful dialogue about some of the cultural differences about where animals fit in with respect to the different categories children identify. For example, dogs are considered dirty and unpleasant by some cultures, while they are beloved family pets in others. Be matter-of-fact about these differences. There is no right or wrong way to view an animal. Avoid putting children on the spot or asking them to speak for their culture. Simply create a safe space for children to express their feelings and consider each other's views.

This discussion may be something you wish to revisit throughout the year and whenever an animal comes to visit the classroom. Encourage the children with frequent conversations about the roles of animals that appear in books or that you encounter on field trips or other excursions.

Although the goal of your discussion should not be to change attitudes, a child who considers a caterpillar a "creepy crawly" animal might change her mind after discussion with a classmate who keeps a caterpillar as a pet. You are not trying to steer anyone to a "right" attitude about animals, but through these discussions you can offer children a context in which to explore their perceptions and feelings about certain animals and the place they hold in children's lives. Perhaps you, the educator, can provide guidance and structure to these discussions. Identifying categories may help us to understand our own feelings about animals and why we seem, collectively and individually, to value some more than others. For more a detailed exploration of this topic, refer to chapter 4.

Dramatic Play

Children often readily identify with animal characters, and they love to play at being animals. Dramatic play can give children an authentic experience of animals by honing their observation, motor, and social skills. It also allows creative and joyful opportunities for perspective taking, empathy, and imagination. When you encourage children to pretend to be animals, they will often relish the opportunity to express themselves in new ways. As most early childhood educators know, dramatic play and dress-up are very important modalities for learning.

- Fill your dramatic play or dress-up area with animal-print fabrics, feathers, and masks. Let children don furred suits, pull on a pair of luminescent butterfly wings, or slip into a shell and become a turtle. Include plenty of mirrors with face paints on ledges beneath them. Allow children to paint their own or their friends' faces to better embody the character of the animal they are becoming. They can immerse themselves fully in imaginative play and dress the part. Open up a space in your classroom (or better yet, outside) where the children can be free to act and play as if they themselves are the animals.

- Use the books and images you've amassed to learn about the animal's body and how it moves. Does it have fins, fur, feathers, scales, or something else? How does it get around? During large-motor time you might put on some fun music and encourage the children to move as "their animal" would move. (Remember, no predation! Animals are not allowed to attack one another, even if they might do so in the wild!)

- Have the children make their own animal costumes. At one school I visited, inspired by David Sobel's book *Beyond Ecophobia*, an art teacher spent time with children creating costumes to depict their chosen animals. They were provided with craft materials, such as cardboard, fabric scraps, and paint, to create costumes. First they designed the costumes, then with the help of parents, volunteers, and teachers, they brought their costumes to life. The only stipulation was that the costumes needed to be products of the children's imagination and their interpretation of their chosen animal. Having spent weeks immersing themselves in learning about these animals, the children really had a sense of what their costumes needed to look like, how they needed to be able to move as animals, and what features were most important. For example, one girl's animal was a bottlenose dolphin, and to her, the most important features of a dolphin's body were its dorsal fin and blowhole, so she spent the most time working on those parts of her costume. Another child, a lemur, knew that he needed a striking ringed tail. Still another child chose a sea turtle as his favorite animal and created a cardboard set of flippers for his costume. The project culminated in a parade through the school, where children were encouraged to move through the school like "their" animal. Parents were invited to attend the parade, and the older children enjoyed seeing their younger friends in beautiful costumes they had created.

- Host a parade, or encourage the children to create dances or skits to perform. Encourage them to act like their "real" animal, rather than creating plays or stories. You want them to really feel as though they are "becoming" the animal, making a connection to that animal through emotion, joy, and pretend play.

When allowed to really engage in this sort of project-based learning activity, or other animal-related projects over time, children will learn a great deal about individual species. Sharing their learning with the other children will be exciting and memorable.

Another way to connect children with animals through dramatic play is the following example, which combines caring experiences with adapting to children's needs. Kim, the director at a child care center, had allergies, as did several of the children in her care. She wanted to have a class pet but knew it would be challenging. Kim decided to build upon the children's love for stuffed animals. On one special day, "Pepper" came to the center. Pepper is a stuffed dog who "lives" at the center. Children are encouraged to cuddle with him when they're having a tough time, they can take him out to play whenever they want to, and he's often part of the learning stations set up in the classroom. Pepper has his own bowl and bed in the classroom, offering children an opportunity to care for him. When they are having snack, Pepper has "snack" also (which consists of scraps of construction paper in his bowl). Each weekend, one child gets to bring him home. He has a journal that travels with him, and during the weekend, the "host family" writes down a note or two about the adventures they've had with Pepper. Often parents will include photos or illustrations documenting their fun as well.

On Monday morning, when Pepper returns, the host child gets a moment to share with the class some tales of what's happened over the weekend. In this way, all children get to share in the "responsibility" of caring for Pepper. Obviously the children know it's not a real dog, but the fun and excitement of getting to "take care" of Pepper for a weekend are thrilling to the children. And having him in the classroom as a comfort measure, someone to play with, read to, cuddle with, or simply talk to, provides a reassuring touch of consistency. Kim reports that "children who might be having a tough time separating in the morning at drop-off can cuddle with Pepper, or during naptime a child may choose to snuggle with him." Pepper is a part of the classroom community and even goes along on field trips or out to the playground. Children remind their teachers to feed him at snacktime, and each child anxiously awaits his turn to take him home over the weekend. Kim's solution is a creative way to offer children a connection with a make-believe companion to care for.

One of the most powerful factors in shaping and supporting a child's exploration of and care and concern for the natural world is the participation of an enthusiastic adult. Any educator or parent who wishes to support children's love for animals and growing sense of stewardship need do nothing more than play, explore, and enjoy having adventures right alongside that child. Simply be present, and share in the joy of discovery with the children. It really does make a difference!

AUTHENTIC EXPERIENCES THROUGH HUMANE EDUCATION

The term *humane education* refers to teaching about what it means to be compassionate, kind, and humane. In many cases, humane education programs specifically focus on animal and environmental issues as well as social justice. While not a set of curricula per se, humane education focuses on

teaching ethics, kindness, gratitude, and compassion. Using a humane-education lens or approach is a natural way to bring children authentic experiences with animals.

Many humane education programs do feature animals as part of the curriculum. These programs offer children opportunities to practice caregiving, develop trust, and learn about integrity, honesty, and kindness. As a part of the curriculum, animals or animal characters factor in to stories or situations that require children to use critical thinking skills and attitudes of humanity and kindness. Children may consider their relationships with animals and are encouraged to talk about their feelings and practices with regard to animal care. Humane education is a great way to introduce children to ethical thinking. Many humane education

programs include opportunities to work together to identify shared ideas about justice, compassion, and empathy. Often they include role-playing activities and other creative ways to encourage children to think about these qualities and practice them. They help children learn to operate in a democratic situation and to welcome others' opinions and feelings. There are many approaches to humane education, and you'll find some of my favorite resources in appendix A, Additional Resources. This approach is yet another way to view animals and support children's authentic animal experiences.

Giving children authentic experiences with animals is a fun and fascinating process. This chapter has covered some approaches, but there are many others, and they often merge together as children's interests grow and change.

A teacher begins a project about canines with an exploration of family pets, dogs belonging to children in the classroom, and stories about dogs the children know or have encountered. Piggybacking on that, the children and their teacher expand the scope of this research, seeking out information about canines that live in their local region, such as coyotes, foxes, and wolves. The children gather as much information about wild canines as possible, which leads to visiting a zoo to see them in real life. The class moves on to exploring abstract representations of the animals, including toys and the many depictions of canines in books and other media. Seeing the children's interest, the teacher helps them write a class book about dogs. He invites the children to bring in stuffed dogs, and they set up a "dog park" in one area of the classroom. The teacher provides loose parts, such as blocks and boxes, and he invites the children to create homes for their dogs. The children have opportunities to demonstrate how they care for their "pets," and this leads to a classroom discussion about caring well for dogs, wolves, foxes, and all animals.

There are so many ways in which you can offer children authentic experiences with animals. From researching animals in the classroom to excursions to zoos or farms, you can help children create tangible, meaningful connections. I hope that this chapter gives you lots of ideas for creating animal connections with children.

6

Animals in the Classroom

Matilda is often the first child to arrive in her classroom each morning, since her mom drops her off on the way to work. She spends the first quiet moments of her morning each day petting and brushing Flopsy, the lop-eared rabbit who lives in the classroom. As the other children enter, some of them quietly come over and join her, visiting and talking to Flopsy. The children socialize together quietly while petting the rabbit and seeing that she has enough food and water for the day. Soon, their teacher rings a bell, and together the children transition into their morning work.

As valuable as interacting with animals in zoos, nature centers, and aquariums is for children, caring for animals directly gives them unique benefits. Providing immediate, daily care to animals can be incredibly stimulating and encouraging for children. Many teachers recognize that having animals in the classroom expands learning opportunities for children and also offers children a chance to practice their social, emotional, and caregiving skills. Finally, animals are beautiful and stimulating to our senses, and they bring us joy! There are plenty of reasons that might motivate you to bring a pet into children's lives. Throughout this chapter, I refer to *classroom pets*, but with this term, I'm also including pets in the homes, offices, or other settings of parents and informal educators who work with children.

One of the most enjoyable things about a classroom pet is simply that it fascinates children. Small "pocket pets" are just the right size for little hands. Reptiles have a texture like no other animals. The quiet movements of fish can be soothing and relaxing. Birds are awe inspiring simply because they can fly. Any animal that is allowed freedom to move about the classroom (safely, under close supervision) of its own accord can instill wonder in

children, just because the animal itself has the power to initiate an interaction. This is a different experience for a child than reaching into a cage and pulling out a guinea pig when the child desires an interaction.

As you read through this chapter, keep in mind that obtaining a classroom pet is a serious commitment. There are safety and health considerations (for both people and animals), maintenance and upkeep, budgetary considerations, curricular connections, and ethical concerns. While this list may seem daunting, I don't want to discourage you. I hope that through reading this book, you've become convinced that children's interactions with animals are valuable and necessary. In this chapter I identify and tackle some of the issues surrounding a classroom pet. I also offer stories from teachers I've worked with. These teachers have used classroom pets to deepen children's learning, to increase understanding of their relationships to one another, and of course, to strengthen the children's bonds to the animals themselves. The more planning you do at the early stages of obtaining a pet, the better your chances of successfully

integrating it into the classroom. Bringing pets (whether household or classroom) into children's lives is well worth the effort and commitment the animals require.

Some critics are justly concerned about classroom pets. Concerns often include stress on the animal from frequent handling and the noise of the classroom environment, and the possibility that an animal's health may fail or that the animal may need emergency care outside of school hours. Others worry about the potential negative health risks to children through exposure to animals. I agree that these factors warrant serious consideration. Any educator or parent considering obtaining an animal must be realistic about the risk involved to both children and animal—as well as about the money, time, and other commitments required to adequately house and care for a classroom pet. But I believe that careful, thoughtful educators can introduce animals to the classroom for the benefit of children while still ensuring that the animals are provided with a high level of sensitive care, attention, and routine health maintenance. Since you're reading this book, it's a good bet you're willing to "go the extra mile" when it comes to providing a safe, comfortable environment for the pet as well as the children.

FINDING A PET

Finding an animal for a classroom takes time, patience, and flexibility. For many educators, the starting point of their journey with children and animals is an "accidental" pet. They may obtain their first classroom pet from a parent or friend who has nowhere else to place it, or they may be given a pet for the classroom by friends or family members from the school community. Some teachers even bring their own pets into the classroom. Whatever the source, many educators find themselves caring for a classroom pet that they did not initially plan on. If this describes your situation, you may be wondering how to make that species of pet work for your classroom. This chapter

CHOOSING THE RIGHT PET

When you decide to obtain a classroom pet, engaging the children in a discussion about the pet is worthwhile. One elementary school teacher, Penny, worked with her class to decide together what kind of pet the children most desired, and which one would be the best companion for the classroom. In anticipation of getting a pet, the children had raised money on their own and collected donations. When Penny realized how committed they were, she engaged them in research to evaluate what animals might make the best candidates for the classroom. "I really wanted to honor their need and desire for a classroom pet," the teacher said, "and I wanted to engage the children in some meaningful research. This was a natural fit." Small groups of students made posters detailing the pros and cons of each pet, and the question was put to a vote. The teacher used the children's money to purchase supplies and materials, and they obtained a bearded dragon for the classroom. The children had invested emotionally and financially in the animal ahead of time and had engaged in academic learning to prepare. In doing so, the children developed a knowledge base about the animal's needs and a shared commitment to caring for the animal and laid a solid groundwork for successful integration of the classroom pet into the students' environment.

offers questions to explore when examining your students' and classroom's needs as well as your pet's needs.

Other educators decide they want a pet and are able to plan, explore options, and research what animal would be the best fit for their situation. Some teachers take a project-based approach, enlisting the children's ideas and engaging them in researching the most likely candidates for a classroom pet while thinking about the pros and cons of each species. If you are considering a classroom pet and are able to explore your options before accepting one, do so!

THINKING ABOUT A CLASSROOM PET

What kinds of animals make good classroom pets? If you ask around, you'll likely get dozens of different responses. The most common classroom pets are birds, gerbils, hamsters, goldfish, guinea pigs, rabbits, reptiles, and amphibians. Some programs with lots of outdoor spaces have goats, horses, llamas, chickens, or even sheep. Although many animal species *can* make good classroom pets, you as an educator need to evaluate your classroom, students, and unique circumstances before bringing an animal into your situation.

Seth, the director of a nature-based preschool, recommends some guiding questions to discuss with children as you think about classroom pets:

- Is the animal real? (This eliminates the dragons and unicorns. Sorry!)

- Is it alive? (This eliminates dinosaurs.)

- Would we be safe if this animal lived with us? (This rules out the giant squid.)

- Would the animal be safe if it lived with us?

- What does this animal need in order to be healthy and happy?

- Would we be able to meet the animal's needs?

Seth suggests narrowing the list to likely contenders. Often one species will rise to the top of the list as the questions are answered. If there is disagreement, you can enlist other classes to help you decide or add criteria such as cost, need for exercise, availability of food, and so on. Below are more points for you to think through, individually and with children, on each of these topics.

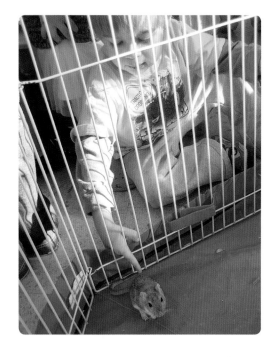

Places to Research and Find Support

Just as you are intentional in your approach to education, you should be intentional about how and where you obtain your pet. Responsibly caring for animals means thoroughly researching whether the animal is a good fit for your program, your budget, the ages of the children you work with, and the amount of time and energy you're willing to commit to its care. I encourage you to research the species beyond the Internet. Visit your local humane society, where you can ask knowledgeable people about that animal. In many places, there are enthusiasts clubs or "rescue organizations" that help place animals in homes or other safe settings. Most animal rescue organizations consist of dedicated volunteers who want to help you find the right fit for your situation. They will work to understand your needs, your setting, and any other considerations to ensure that you and the animal are a good match. They can also help alleviate the concern some people may feel about taking in "abused" and potentially unpredictable animals. A rescue organization will help you find an animal that will adjust to the active, sometimes noisy classroom setting.

For example, in my area of the Twin Cities in Minnesota, there is a reptile and amphibian club. They have monthly meetings, a speakers bureau, and volunteers who help prospective owners research and choose the most appropriate animal for a classroom. The club offers a wealth of information about reptile and amphibian care—more than I could hope to gain browsing in a "pets section" in my local bookstore. And the dedication, personal experience, and knowledge offered by the volunteers ensure I'll get much better information than I might with a random Internet search. Getting involved with a local club is a great way to learn more about your potential pet as well as other, similar species. There are often clubs for reptiles and amphibians (together this group is known as *herptiles* or *herps* for short), rabbits, chinchillas, tropical fish, and "pocket pets"—those small furry creatures like mice, gerbils, and hamsters that look as if they'd fit in a pocket (but should *never* be carried around in one!). Check the Internet to see what clubs exist in your area. An enthusiasts club can also be a source of support. In addition to helping you learn more about the animal species, volunteers may be available to assist you in resolving any issues that arise.

Another source of information are local veterinarians. They can provide you with detailed information on how best to care for your animal and give you a general sense of how much money you'll need to be prepared to spend on the animal over the course of its lifetime. Expenses will obviously include food and housing for the animal, but some animals require, for example, annual checkups, vitamin supplements, specialized lights or heat sources, treats, or toys.

Don't forget to include your coworkers in the decision as well. Although the children will have an active role in the care and feeding of your classroom pet, you will ultimately be responsible for the animal's health and well-being. Inevitably you will go on vacation, have a sick day, or need a backup caregiver for some other reason, so coworkers should be on board with your plans! You will also want to know about any staff member's concerns or fears. If you had hoped to obtain a corn snake for the classroom and a teacher down the hall is terrified of snakes, you might decide to reconsider the animal you choose, out of respect for the teacher. On the other hand, if you have coworkers who are squeamish about snakes, a classroom snake could be a great learning opportunity for everyone and give them a chance to grow beyond their discomfort. Be open to discussing your choice with other teachers. Welcome their feedback, and hear their concerns. Respect their feelings and fears. In some cases, obtaining an animal that not everyone's comfortable with can provide a really valuable tool for personal growth. Remind your coworkers that their attitudes will be reflected in the children's attitudes. Be positive and ensure that everyone's comfortable with the animal you select.

Finally, ask around the school community. Perhaps there are families or teachers involved with your program who already own a pet bird (for example) and would be happy to coach you through the initial phase. You can benefit from their experience: ask them about any unexpected expenses or other surprises that they've encountered, so that you may be better prepared for a smooth and easy transition.

One final thought on resources for obtaining a pet: when you decide to obtain an animal, be sure it is coming from a source that is responsible in its care and husbandry of animals. Unfortunately, some animal breeders subject their animals to inhumane conditions, overcrowding, and highly stressful situations. Often, pet stores obtain their "merchandise" from these breeders, thereby supporting and perpetuating the inhumane conditions. Not only is this inhumane treatment simply unethical, but the stress and anxiety created by these conditions can also result in unhealthy or unpredictable animals. You should also be aware of the laws regarding wildlife in your area. Although you may be able to obtain some species from suppliers, pet stores, and anonymous vendors on the Internet, local laws regarding these species may make their possession illegal. For example, possession of red-eared slider turtles is illegal in some states, although they're sold in pet stores in those very same states. Again, connect with an

> At a nature center where I once worked, a fellow naturalist was very uncomfortable with helping to care for a snake we had on exhibit, due to his own fears and misconceptions about snakes. He recognized, however, the necessity of participating in its care and well-being (after all, animal care was part of his job!). Little by little, he gradually overcame his fear and eventually developed a strong love of reptiles, even leading programs and classes about reptiles for children. Adults, like children, need a chance to overcome their fears and discomfort.

enthusiasts club or rescue organization: they can help you find an animal from a reputable source.

As you think about what kind of animal might be the best fit for your setting, I encourage you to refer to appendix B, the Classroom Pet Care Checklist. This list will help you get started in your research. It addresses basic questions about topics such as care and feeding and health considerations. Of course, this list is by no means exhaustive, and you should seek out specific expert advice on the animal species you are considering. Other good sources of information are local nature centers, local branches of the Humane Society, pet rescue organizations, NAEYC's *Young Children* magazine, and the National Science Teachers Association. Check out the resources listed in appendix A, Additional Resources, for more ways to support your animal search.

Basic Needs and Costs

As you begin researching an animal, you'll need to answer logistical questions about your pet's daily living and care. Engage the children in a discussion: Will we all be involved in the animal's care, or just the teachers? What are the animal's basic needs? This is a great way to engage children in informal research. You can identify together what needs the animal has for care and feeding. Use your local library and the Internet. Visit a pet store together, and talk with the workers there about what your prospective pet will need. Perhaps ask a parent or community member who owns an animal of that species (or similar) to come and talk about caring for it.

You'll need to consider the animal's feeding requirements. What does it eat? Where and how often do you need to obtain food for the pet? Does its food require refrigeration (for example, fresh fruits and vegetables, or frozen meat)?

All animals require fresh drinking water, though some require more than others. Be sure that you understand how frequently you need to provide water to your pet. Does the pet require a water bottle, a dish of fresh water, or something else? Does your pet also get its water through fresh foods such as fruits and vegetables? If you choose to have fish, there are a number of important considerations when preparing a tank, whether freshwater or saltwater. Consult a fish expert in your area for guidance on preparing and maintaining a fish tank. It can be more challenging than it looks!

Be aware that many animal foods contain peanuts and tree nuts. Some may contain shellfish, wheat, or even egg protein. While children will never be consuming animal feed, if they are enlisted in care and feeding of the animal, they will most certainly come into contact with these potential allergens. Furthermore, simply having the food around may create unsafe conditions (food dust, debris, packaging) for children who are extremely sensitive to these allergens. Most animal foods are available without these common allergens. If parents donate animal food, be sure that they are aware of this concern. While you may not have an allergic child in your classroom at the moment, the incidence of childhood food allergies is high. Take the time to find animal food that is free of common allergens so that you can have an inclusive classroom and avoid risks to children who may be allergic.

How will you provide adequate opportunities for the animal to get exercise and meet its other physical needs? Will it roam freely throughout the classroom or another designated space? Rodents may use "hamster wheels" for exercise, but they will need opportunities to climb, burrow, and walk around as well. How will you provide these opportunities? Some animals need to chew or gnaw, so you'll want to offer them appropriate materials to chew on.

Also, identify your pet's need for privacy, a "sleeping area" if you will. All creatures need a space to get away from it all, and small classroom pets are no exception. One thing I've seen some educators do well is ensure that animals have a space to "get away from it all" in a constructed cave or other sheltered space. Be sure you can provide an appropriate "hiding place" for your pet, be it a nest box, hollow log, or even a plastic princess castle, if you must. Just make sure your animal has a place where it can go when it needs a break from the action. (I've also seen a gerbil cage on a low table in the middle of the classroom, with no "hide box" or walled shelter inside where the gerbil could get away from the curious eyes and hands of the children. A stressful life indeed.) Animals, like people, need to be able to have quiet places, where they won't be disturbed, for rest, solitude, and comfort. Consider, too, whether the animal you are interested in is nocturnal (mostly active at night). If so, will it be sleeping throughout the day, when the children are there?

Consider the habitat requirements for the animal. You may decide on a gerbil and find an inexpensive small plastic tank to fit on a shelf, but can you possibly get larger accommodations for the animal? Again, consider the animal's well-being. You want to create the best home possible for the animal. Research the animal's space requirements, and make sure you will be able to provide it with as much space as possible. How can you make that happen? Buy a large tank or cage, enlist a willing and handy parent volunteer to build something, or, if your local climate allows, create an outdoor home that will provide the animal with plenty of safe space to roam.

Consider where you're going to put your animal. If you have a small animal like a rodent or turtle, you'll want to put the cage or tank on a low shelf to ensure children have access to it, but you'll also need to make sure that children will be supervised in their interactions with the pet. If your pet is kept high on a shelf, away from the children's reach, the children will miss out on many wonderful opportunities to see and connect with the pet. Conversely, if the animal is kept on a low table in the middle of everything, constantly within reach of children and with no place to get away, it may begin to show signs of stress or anxiety. Look around your classroom, and

be sure that you have a place that allows the animal a bit of space from everyday goings-on but is also accessible to the children. Ensure that the animal's home is placed where there's no danger of it being knocked off or having things dropped on or into it. Involve the children in finding a special and safe spot for the animal's tank or cage in the classroom.

Consider the animal's requirements for heat, electricity, and light. Do you need to place the animal near electrical outlets or near a window? Be sure it's not positioned directly beneath a warm or cold air vent or under a drafty window, or the animal may become ill. Pay close attention to the animal's requirements for temperature, light, and other environmental conditions. Consult with experts, and do your homework so you can be sure you are providing the animal with what it needs to be healthy and comfortable.

Remember that adults send many messages about animals through the way we talk about and treat them. Even something as seemingly uncomplicated as figuring out where to place the animal in the classroom and how its living quarters are maintained can communicate a lot about that animal's worth and value. Consider the message that is sent to children in this example: A solitary goldfish is kept in a grungy tank that is rarely cleaned. Scum is built up on the inside of the glass, and there is little light. The goldfish tank is high on a shelf, and the teacher sometimes forgets to feed the fish. What does that communicate about the worth and value of the fish?

When you decide to get a classroom pet, the children will be very excited and want to be as involved as possible. This is great! Work together to create a list of the jobs that will be shared by the children, and post it near where you'll keep the animal. Be sure that the animal's cage or tank will be located in a prominent location where the children will have easy access to it. Ensure that the children are familiar with how to operate the doors or other opening on the pet's enclosure. This will avoid pinched fingers and other mishaps during the transfer of the pet to and from its enclosure. Set clear rules about when and if the children will have access to the animal, and establish rules about when and how the pet will be handled or touched. Make it a part of your morning routine to check on the animal, ensuring its cage or tank is clean and it has food and plenty of water.

You will also need to provide the animal with regular veterinary checkups, and this will cost money. Do you have a budget for this? How will you secure and sustain funding for pet care? Will you take donations, hold a children's art sale, or host some other kind of classroom fundraiser? Perhaps there is a parent in your school community who is a veterinarian whom you could work with at a discount. Occasionally, the animal may need emergency veterinarian care, such as if it becomes ill or suffers a fall or some other mishap. How will this be handled?

Of course, you'll also need to be sure that you're keeping your pet happy and taking care of its emotional needs. Be sure to monitor the children's activity and make your expectations clear so that the animal doesn't become overly stressed from noise or from being handled. Animals who are stressed become very anxious, and signs of stress or anxiety vary depending on the species. Some common examples of an animal's anxious behaviors include repetitive chewing or licking of its own tail or limbs, excessive digging, pacing back and forth, screeching or other distressed noises, pecking, nipping, or chewing on its own paws, tail, or other animals in the cage, and biting children. If any of these behaviors crop up during your pet's lifetime in the classroom, you need to reevaluate how you're handling the pet, where it's placed, and its level of involvement with the children. Rather than immediately deciding that "a classroom pet just won't work for me!" use the situation as a teachable moment. Talk with the children about stress and anxiety and how animals show that. Ask them to consider what might need to be changed. Reexamine your class rules about the pet. What's not working? Are the children too free to grab at the animal with little or no supervision? Is the animal simply subjected to too much activity? Think about your pet's living conditions and housing setup. Are you meeting its needs adequately? Perhaps there is something missing in the animal's diet? Are there multiple pets? Maybe the mix of gender, number of pets, or species isn't quite working. Be sure to get the animal thoroughly checked by a vet to ensure there's no underlying health problem present. Remember your commitment to the animal and the children. Although the situation can be frustrating, often a little concentrated attention to detail will help you iron out difficulties the animal is experiencing before they develop into a serious problem.

Planning Long-Term

Even if you plan to engage the children directly in the majority of the animal's care, ultimately you are responsible for its well-being. You must be willing to provide a home for the animal for the duration of its life or have a plan in place to send the animal to a caregiver who can. Again, before obtaining any living creatures, please do your homework and have a plan.

Make sure that caring for your pet is never an afterthought. Consider how your pet will be integrated into the day-to-day operations at your center. Who will be the pet's primary caregiver? Regardless of the amount of care the children are involved in, you need to establish a responsible adult as the animal's primary care provider who can oversee cleaning and feeding schedules, keep tabs on the pet's health and possibly provide emergency care, and see to other details. Will it be you? A team of teachers? How will you ensure your pet has continuity of care, for example, on the weekends or during other school breaks? How will you engage coworkers, including custodial staff, in caring for the pet? Although they may not be directly involved in caring for the animal, they should definitely be made aware of special considerations. For example, many cleaning sprays and chemicals used in the classroom emit vapors or leave residue that may be harmful for animals, and it's important to communicate this to those involved in cleaning and maintenance of your school or center.

You must have a plan in place for how the animal will be cared for during breaks, such as weekends, holidays, and summer vacation. You may need to go to your center to ensure the animal has fresh water and food daily. What if you leave your center through retirement or a job change? Will the animal go with you, or will you appoint another teacher and show him how to care for it? Many of us may pleasantly recall our own childhood experiences of being appointed the "weekend babysitter" for a classroom pet. In actuality, sending a classroom pet home with a different child each week is never a good idea. Going to a new environment so frequently can be extremely stressful for the animal. The changes a small animal experiences can be overwhelming. A new setting each weekend has new temperatures and surroundings to get used to. If smokers live in the house, the animal may be harmed by second-hand smoke. A pet, such as a dog or cat, may be intensely curious about the visitor, creating extreme fear and anxiety. Younger or older children in the home who haven't been taught how to handle the animal may get too rough. The family might be very busy and neglect to feed it. Or noise in the house may frighten the pet. Subjecting a classroom pet to this many variables each weekend is best avoided.

You should also consider the impact that an injury to or death of an animal would have on a child who had been entrusted with its care for a weekend. An accident resulting in injury or loss of life to a classroom pet can result in tremendous guilt on the part of the offending family, most specifically the child.

Continuity of care is one of the most important considerations for any educator wishing to bring a pet into the classroom. You simply must have a plan in place to care for the animal throughout its entire life span. This includes weekends. This includes summer break. This includes your own vacation time. This even includes a job change.

What if, despite your best efforts, it simply doesn't work out to keep a classroom pet? Most small animals are very difficult to find homes for. Your backup plan should include a second home for the animal. Again, families in your program, rescue organizations, and enthusiasts clubs will be a great source of support in your backup plan, so it pays to get involved. If the worst happens, and you find that for some reason you cannot keep the animal in the classroom, you need to have a plan for its care. Under no circumstances should a classroom pet be released into the wild. This will endanger the life of your animal and can cause great damage to native wildlife communities.

The term *native* is applied to wildlife populations to describe animals that have historically occurred in a local ecological community. These animals have evolved alongside other populations and have established local food sources, developed resistance to local pathogens and disease-causing organisms, and are part of a food web. When introduced, nonnative animal species can prey upon native animals, bring previously unknown pathogens to native populations, and disrupt a balanced ecological community. In many cases nonnative species have no natural predators, which means that their population will multiply very quickly before native populations can adapt. Animals such as the popular African clawed frog and red-eared slider turtle (and some other reptile, amphibian, and insect species that may be obtained by mail order) can cause serious disruptions in native populations. These animals are not indigenous to many regions of the United States and should not be released into the wild at the end of the study period. In fact, releasing *any* animals into the wild is illegal in most states.

Even the most unlikely animal can cause major problems. For example, did you know that the common brown earthworm, a favorite classroom animal, is not native to many parts of North America? It's true. Although they are all but ubiquitous these days, earthworms were not historically residents of North American soils until relatively recently. They were introduced to most North American forests by human activity such as construction and road building, and through the well-intentioned but harmful actions of anglers who released leftover fishing bait onto the forest floor. Every gardener knows that earthworms can be great for the garden: Their manure, or "castings," fertilizes and enriches the soil. They burrow through the dirt, aerating it and loosening it. But too much of a good thing can be dreadful. Earthworms reproduce quickly. They lay thousands of eggs. And earthworms eat "duff"— that earthy mixture of fallen leaves, decaying wood, and other natural materials on the forest floor. As earthworms chew through the plant roots and other vegetation, they change the soil content and affect its structure. In doing so, they alter the food web and habitat of countless other organisms found in the top layer of soils.

Now scientists recognize the "earthworm invasion" as a case where a population of nonnative animals spun out of control and has had deleterious

continued

effects on an entire ecological system. The makeup of the soil is hugely impacted by the actions of earthworms. Of course, the earthworm invasion was not caused by one kindergarten teacher who dumped a coffee can of worms into the park behind her school. It's a long-term effect caused by many things over several decades. But the effect has had a lasting impact on forest and soil ecosystems, plant communities, and food webs. It provides a real-life and very striking example of how the introduction of a seemingly benign creature to a nonnative habitat can have a negative ripple effect.

Here's a second example of small animals having large effects. Some teachers choose to purchase populations of bullfrog tadpoles. Witnessing firsthand the cycle of growth and metamorphosis can leave a lasting impression and sense of wonder in many children, and many naturalists and scientists recall just such experiences in their childhood as those moments that "turned them on" to science. Unfortunately, when a teacher is finished with the project, unless she has made plans for the adult frogs, she may be tempted to simply release them into the local pond. It seems like a simple solution, and if bullfrogs are native to her area, what's the problem, anyway?

There are a couple of potentially negative effects that may result from such a move. First, the frogs may introduce unwanted pathogens and bacteria to the local amphibian population. If the bullfrogs used in the classroom came from a pond far from where the classroom is located, they will be physiologically adapted to a certain microclimate (that is, a particular "slice" of a habitat or ecological region) or even the laboratory where they were grown. When the adult animals are released, they carry with them bacteria and other microorganisms that may or may not have previously existed in the pond. These can create health problems for native species. The second effect is much more common, similar to the earthworm example above. If the bullfrogs are released into an area where they have no natural predators, suddenly they become the "apex" predator, that is, the top of the local food chain. Bullfrogs in fact are quite formidable predators and feed on small mammals, ducklings, smaller frogs, toads, and fish. Introduction of a new predator to an ecological community can be devastating to local populations. Even if an animal is native to an area, it may not be native to the specific pond, field, or forest where it is released, and it can cause a major disruption of the local ecosystem.

continued

Although it's tempting to purchase caterpillars or tadpoles through mail-order sources, use them for a class project, and then release them, I discourage educators and parents from doing so. While releasing butterflies and frogs may seem harmless, I hope the examples I've provided will show the "ripple effect" that this practice can have.

If you find there are issues that you just cannot resolve on your own or with the help of other resources, and you find you simply cannot keep your pet, make sure you follow through on your commitment to care for the animal. Individual circumstances will dictate the appropriate next steps, but there are always humane and responsible ways to find new homes for animals that just don't work out in the classroom. Ask around your school community for parents or other teachers who might be able to adopt the animal. Contact a local rescue organization or enthusiasts club for assistance in finding a home for your pet. Ask veterinarians and others who care for animals if they can help you find a home. Finally, check with one of the many online communities that are committed to helping pet owners responsibly find homes for pets. (A short list of these is in appendix A, Additional Resources.) Please make sure that your commitment to finding the animal a good home is upheld. It may take a while, but if you've done your research and engaged your coworkers and others in your community, you will not be without support and resources.

Health and Safety

Other important considerations include health and safety, for the animals and for the children. Most educators and parents have concerns about pathogens and disease that an animal might carry, such as *Salmonella*. Adults should *always* supervise children's hand washing after contact with animals to ensure the children use soap and wash thoroughly.

Not only should hands that have touched an animal directly be washed, but also hands that have touched animal food dishes, water dishes, cages, tanks, or toys. Pathogens are transmitted through contact with any of these items. Items associated with animal care (for example, animal food dishes) should always be washed in a sink that is not used for food preparation, since bacteria can splash onto nearby countertops, dishcloths, and towels. Keep animal food dishes well away from any eating areas. And be sure you have cleaning supplies (brushes, sponges, buckets) that are exclusively for use in animal care—don't ever use a scrub brush to clean an animal's tank and then later wipe a child's chair or table (including sensory tables) with that brush. Never mix chemicals or cleaning supplies in a bucket that you'll use for animal care. Clearly label with permanent marker all animal supplies as for "Animal Care Only" so that no one makes any mistakes. Many educators and caregivers also choose to wear rubber gloves when cleaning out animal tanks, changing bedding, and rinsing food and water dishes. Keep your animal care supplies well away from other cleaning and maintenance supplies.

I mention these risks not to scare you or deter you from obtaining a classroom pet. But it's important that you recognize the level of commitment and the possible hazards and risks involved in keeping a pet in a classroom. You should have accurate and current information about health risks associated with common pets in order to answer parents' many questions. Parents may not know much about disease-causing bacteria such as *Salmonella* and *E. coli*, and you can inform them with up-to-date accurate information about these bacteria and other animal-related health risks. None of the health risks preclude educators from having classroom pets. They just require you to do your homework and take the necessary precautions to ensure the health and safety of the children in your care.

A NOTE ABOUT *SALMONELLA*

Salmonella is often associated with food-borne illness; however, the bacteria are also carried by birds and reptiles. Reptiles shed it in their feces. Birds, including chicks and ducklings (common classroom pets), occasionally carry the disease. *Salmonella* causes diarrhea, stomach upset, and occasionally vomiting, and in rare cases, it can lead to hospitalization. For this reason, the Centers for Disease Control and Prevention discourages children under five from handling reptiles or birds. Children and adults should always wash their hands with soap and water immediately after handling *any* animal, its environment, food and water dishes, or bedding, but these species in particular require extra precautions.

Two excellent resources are the Centers for Disease Control and Prevention (CDC) and the American Academy of Pediatrics. (You can find their websites in appendix A, Additional Resources.) The CDC offers a wealth of information about animals and their associated health risks for young children, including the website "Healthy Pets, Healthy People," which has educational materials, such as posters and pamphlets encouraging hand washing, and other important information regarding children and animals. The American Academy of Pediatrics also offers a host of articles and webcasts related to pets and animals and their effects on children's health.

Other health concerns include dealing with children's allergies, children's sensitivity to animal food or bedding (for example, children with nut allergies should not be exposed to many types of rodent or bird food), and children with asthma (who may react to bedding material that is dusty or fibrous, such as sawdust or fine clay). Be aware that some animal species are triggers for asthma or other respiratory problems. As you choose a pet, find out which pets produce the most dander (minute flakes of dead skin cells) and which pets molt (lose feathers) and decide whether those animals will be a good fit for your classroom. Many animals who produce even a small amount of dander may be asthma triggers for children with allergies to animal dander. And feathers that are frequently shed, ruffled, or preened also have dander. Even if those children "outgrow" your program, you can be sure more children with asthma will enter, as the rate of childhood asthma continues to rise.

Many parents worry that their child will be bitten by an animal, and you'll need to address these concerns. While most domesticated animals that are suitable for learning environments are relatively nonaggressive, all animals have the potential to bite or scratch at little hands when they feel threatened. In many cases, this behavior is a pet's only defense mechanism. Ensuring that the children are holding and touching an animal respectfully and carefully and not crowding it or being loud are some ways you can manage the animal's experience so that it does not feel threatened. Which leads to the next point: as mentioned earlier, consider the animal's health and safety as well. You'll need to ensure that while the children are learning how to handle the pet, you can be there to closely supervise their handling and touching of the pet.

CHILDREN'S LEARNING AND INVOLVEMENT

When an early childhood program has resident animals, children reap the rewards—and in many cases, so do the animals! Children love to participate in caring for animals, doing everything from feeding and watering to assisting with cage and tank cleaning and more. Often, children bring special treats for classroom pets such as carrots, paper towel tubes, fresh berries, or even "decorations" and pictures they've created for the pet.

Planning for Children's Development

As most early childhood educators know, meaningful work is the best way for children to become invested in something. And it's easier than you may think to offer children meaningful ways to participate in caring for animals. Although some educators, out of concern for the animals or the children themselves, are tempted to limit children's involvement to simply "checking on" or watching the classroom animals, when children are offered meaningful work, they tend to be more deeply engaged in their outcome. By "meaningful work," I'm referring to work related to the animal's care that will help it grow and thrive. Everyday chores such as feeding the animal, changing its water, and cleaning its tank offer children a way to be directly involved in the animal's basic needs.

As you involve the children in significant care with the animal, think about other aspects of children's learning. What are your educational goals and objectives related to caring for a pet? How will its care be a part of your curriculum? Will the animal be there as a companion and to help children develop socially and emotionally? Maybe all of the above? Just as you plan your classroom activities and physical environment mindfully and thoughtfully, do the same with your plans for a classroom pet. How do you plan to involve the animal in the children's learning? How do you plan to involve the children in caring for the animal? What will you do to enrich the children's relationships with the pet? How will you ensure the pet is properly cared for and healthy? Spend some time researching the curricular connections in this book, and think about the application of humane education programs (as described in chapter 5) and how your classroom pet might support efforts

in that area. Consider the different learning disciplines such as math, science, and language arts. Chapter 5 included some ideas for planning animal-focused lessons and activities in these domains. How might a live classroom pet help make those lessons more meaningful?

An example from a kindergarten class demonstrates several ways to support children's learning with animals. The class was home to a cockatiel, Ringo, who had freedom to fly inside the classroom and move of her own accord (her wings were clipped, but she could fly for short distances). The teacher, Marshall, helped the children recognize the specialness of Ringo by pointing out to them, "We need her companionship, and she needs ours as well. How can we take good care of her?" This sort of question engages children immediately. Instead of assigning children a list of chores involved in caring for Ringo, this conversation encouraged the children to think about the bird in terms of her needs and to consider how to keep her happy and healthy.

The question "What do you think our bird needs?" formed the basis for many discussions and conversations about the pet's physical and emotional needs. Many children were able to identify the physical needs their bird would have, for example, a place to roost at night and sleep, a food dish, a source of water, the ability to move around freely, and a place to hide. Children were engaged in identifying the bird's basic needs and ensuring they could meet those needs. They did this partially by identifying their own basic needs and how their needs are met in their own homes. In doing so, the children were learning and demonstrating empathy.

In exploring the bird's need for food, the children had the opportunity to research what birds eat. In addition to providing her with birdseed, they grew sprouts to feed to Ringo. This caring act of growing food specifically for the cockatiel helped the children develop patience, because they had to wait for the sprouts to grow. They had to tend to the sprouts over the course of several days, which strengthened their attention to this seemingly long-term project. And they had to put the bird's need for food ahead of their own needs or desires to play when they chose to water and tend to the growing sprouts during their choice time at school. When the bird responded by eating the sprouts, they were encouraged in their efforts.

Marshall asked the children other questions, too, in order to deepen their relationships with Ringo. The questions were designed to provoke children's thinking, such as "Do you think birds get bored? How can we keep her happy?" These kinds of questions led the children to think more deeply about the emotional well-being of the bird, practicing empathy and perspective-taking skills. The children needed to reflect on how they saw the bird behaving. Did she seem bored? They needed to consider their own understanding of what boredom is and how a bird might express that feeling. They needed to consider the behavior they'd seen her exhibiting and think about whether this matched their expectations of what a bored bird might do. The children had to align their understanding of how a bird might experience boredom with how they themselves experience boredom. This further clarified the children's experience of Ringo being "like me, but different" in their learning about the world.

In thinking about her happiness or boredom, the children also needed to consider the bird's everyday behavior. What had they seen her doing? How did they know what she liked or didn't like? They thought about what they had seen her doing and what sorts of things they had seen her avoiding. (For example, she didn't go to the sensory table or perch near the door to the hallway.) Several of the children knew that she liked to perch on different things, so they spent their choice time creating decorative perches for Ringo. Many of them spent time creating entertainment for the bird, such as fancy perches with bells and decorations.

Over the course of several weeks, the children noticed that she seemed to prefer some perches over others in the classroom. This led to an in-depth exploration in which the children tested their ideas about what different surfaces she might prefer. Based on what they'd seen her perching on before, they were able to make predictions about what she might like and be most likely to use. The children made a variety of different perches and made them available to Ringo. They could observe which perches she chose and speculate about why. This led to observations about things such as texture, size and width, color, placement, and other characteristics of the perches the bird had to choose from.

These children's interaction with Ringo is a great example of how caring for an animal can lead not only to emotional growth but also to academic growth. The children were challenged to think scientifically about their questions (What kind of perches does Ringo like? How do we know?) when they made observations and predictions about what Ringo would like and use. As they observed her behavior with the perches, they drew conclusions using a basic scientific method.

Dealing with Death

Inevitably, if you have a classroom pet, the pet will eventually die. There are countless ways that a classroom pet can die, but the fact is, they all do. As an educator, it's worth taking some time to think about how you, personally and professionally, want to handle the deaths of animals, and how you plan to communicate with children about it. There are all kinds of approaches to handling an animal's death, and this section covers a few of them.

One educator I knew was surprised when he approached his classroom's fish tank one morning to find the classroom goldfish floating, dead, in the water. He didn't have time to consider or plan his reaction, because the children saw it at about the same time he did. Naturally, they were alarmed and full of questions. The teacher didn't know how to respond, and he didn't feel it was his place to talk to the children about death. He didn't want them to see the fish, but they had, and now they had questions. The teacher, feeling "put on the spot" and not sure how to respond, told the children what many adults might be inclined to say, "Goldie went to sleep." Of course, this response was met with more questions, such as, "Why won't Goldie wake up?" and "What if I don't wake up?" Unfortunately, the teacher's attempt to brush off their questions about death backfired. It was, for many of the children, their first experience with death. The teacher wasn't sure how to respond to their questions upon seeing the dead fish, and he was stuck with having to come up with a response very quickly without having time to think about it. He felt that he needed to "respect the children's religious beliefs" and not say anything about death that might be contrary to what the children's families might believe. However, in overtly avoiding the topic of death, he was forced to come up with a euphemism, that the fish "went to sleep," which resulted in a whole new set of questions and anxieties. The idea of falling asleep and not waking up can be terrifying for young children, and in the students' minds, it suddenly became a real possibility! It had happened to the fish. They had seen it with their own eyes.

The lesson here is to always be prepared. Consider, even before you bring an animal to the classroom, how you're going to handle the inevitable questions about death. Even if you get an animal that is expected to live for a very long time, such as a bird or reptile, prepare yourself. Unexpected things happen. Animals become ill, and accidents occur.

Think about the factors that will affect your response and how they may change based on students and circumstances. Are you in a faith-based or secular program? Have the children's parents expressed their preferences to you? How can you defer to parents and let them provide their own explanations without ignoring or dismissing the children's questions? How can you create a respectful "memorial" to the animal that honors the possibly diverse beliefs and perspectives of your classroom? How can you talk comfortably about death if the children's ideas aren't the same as your own?

An example of another approach is from Marshall, the kindergarten teacher who had Ringo the bird. One morning, he arrived to the kindergarten classroom to find the bird dead on the floor of the cage. The children were just arriving for the day, and he quickly removed the bird's body and placed it in a box. During the class's morning meeting, he gathered the children together and told them he had found the bird dead and that he was sad. He wanted to give the children space to share their feelings and ask their questions, and he was sensitive to the fact that not all the children in the class shared the same religious beliefs. He felt it was important to share with the children the truth about what had happened (that he had found the bird dead) and that he was feeling sad. This gave the children permission to feel sad as well.

He invited the children to talk about their feelings and ask questions but didn't require anyone to share their feelings. Some of the children said that they were sad, too; others didn't say much. When one boy stated that the bird was "in heaven now," Marshall honored the boy's belief and that of others by responding, "That sounds like something your family believes very strongly, and many families share that belief. Other families believe other things. Would anyone like to share another belief they might have?" He didn't put anyone on the spot, nor did he discount any particular child's questions or beliefs. He simply opened up a safe space for the children to have a conversation and to share their feelings. Other children simply wanted to be quiet, and he respectfully allowed them the space to *not* speak, as this was how they needed to process what had happened. Marshall describes this as "holding the space for them to have a dialogue together"—he offered them an opportunity to practice listening to one another, being vulnerable together, and feeling sad together.

When the bird died, rather than talking about its afterlife or brushing off their questions, this teacher allowed the children space to talk about it and welcomed their questions. He didn't dismiss anyone's questions about the afterlife; he simply let them share their feelings and thoughts. He kept the discussion respectful and helped the children express and experience their feelings of grief, confusion, and surprise about the bird's death. Marshall knew that some children would be fearful of seeing the dead bird, so he had placed its body in a box. He invited any children who wanted to see her body to stay for a moment at pick-up time to look at her. He knew most of the children's caregivers would be there at that time as well. Several of the children chose to look at her body and say a final good-bye. Throughout the week, during choice time, many of the children created cards, pictures, or letters for the bird, which they placed on her cage as a sort of memorial to her.

There are many ways to honor a pet's memory, and it's natural to want to share memories of why a pet was special. When a classroom pet dies, inviting the children to create art, cards and letters, or other creative expressions of their love for the pet can be a helpful way to let children say good-bye. You may save these pieces and create a classroom poster or memorial wall, or you may bind them all together in a special book. Perhaps you could have the children each bring their memorial home to share with their parents, where they can have a more individual conversation that includes their own religious or spiritual beliefs about what happens after death. Making memorial posters, books, and cards and planting memorial gardens can be very healing for children. You may also decide to have a memorial service or "funeral" of sorts. Older children may write special poems or elegies for the dead animal, and you can create a special event with quiet music and

a chance for the children to say their final good-byes. Perhaps a parent who plays an instrument can come in and play the music during your service. You can encourage the children to share their feelings about the animal and to be respectful of each other's feelings; this builds a sense of community and gentleness. A service need not be religious in nature; you can keep the tone focused on an appreciation of the animal and why it was so special to the children.

When a classroom pet dies, the important thing is to be honest with the children. Knowing that you, too, have feelings about the animal dying can be tremendously reassuring for them. Remind the children that some people may feel sad, and others may not. If you don't address the feelings associated with the very real loss, you may be sending a subtle message to the children that their feelings don't matter. Be honest and be prepared. Let the children have their feelings. If you aren't comfortable with religious implications or undertones present, simply mention that different families may believe different things, and invite other children to share their feelings or beliefs. Keep the tone respectful, and don't allow arguing. Most children will not argue with each other over faith and spirituality; they are great listeners and can create a welcoming environment for each other to share their feelings.

One five-year-old boy was devastated when his pet goldfish died suddenly one day. He cried and cried and was given space to share his feelings and sadness. At the end of the day, he taped a picture of a goldfish to the wall above his bed. "Whenever I feel sad about Swimmy dying," he said, "I'm going to kiss this picture."

Some children may draw pictures. Others may place flowers or special stones near an animal's grave or other special place set aside in the home or classroom to memorialize the animal. These are all appropriate ways to mark the occasion, and they help children honor the love and loss they feel. They also send the message to children that their feelings are okay and that the classroom setting is a safe place for them to have their feelings. When a familiar or beloved pet dies, all children will experience grief. Their grief, however, is not necessarily the same cognitive or emotional experience that an adult experiences. Grief is a very individual thing, and there is no one right way to respond.

For many children, the death of a beloved pet, classroom or otherwise, is the first experience they have with death. There will naturally be lots of questions and likely many tears. The children will have many feelings to sort out, and they will need help doing so. They may experience denial, sadness, anger, and confusion. I advise you to reach out to parents when the classroom pet dies. Many children will feel real trauma at the loss of a classroom pet to which they have become very attached. Sometimes their feelings don't show up until later. They may have trouble sleeping or have bad dreams. Sometimes they regress and have toileting issues. You should let the parents know that the pet has died and should tell them about how the class handled the occasion.

As an educator, you may find this situation to be very challenging. How do you make space for the children's emotions and support them in their grief, while respecting the many cultural beliefs and values about death and what comes after? I can't provide easy answers for you, but I hope the experiences shared above give you some food for thought as you consider different ways you can support children in dealing with an animal's death.

I do suggest that although it may be uncomfortable for you, that you make time and space during the days following an animal's death for the children to talk about it. Some children will want to talk about it; others may not. This is okay. Resist the urge to push those children who aren't yet ready to talk about it. Allow those who are ready to discuss the animal's death to talk with one another, sharing their questions, their feelings, and their memories of the pet. This is a time when children practice saying a final good-bye. It's okay for you to answer, "I don't know" to their questions, if this is the truth. Remember to resist the urge to say that an animal was "put to sleep" or "died in its sleep," as these terms are euphemistic and can create lots of fear and anxiety in children.

Faith-based settings will likely have a plan or program in place that presents a unified response about death. In this case, you will want to follow the established plan, but be aware that the children will not know the plan and will likely still have lots of questions and feelings that they need help to process. You can stay true to your program's religious convictions and still honor the children's needs.

BRINGING IN TEMPORARY PETS

Many educators who wish to host a classroom pet are unable to do so, and instead choose to "adopt" pets or introduce live animals in other ways. In an effort to have live animals without the many challenges presented by reptiles, pocket pets, and others, many teachers choose to raise insects or arthropods in their classroom. This can be a great way to involve children in the care and feeding of living creatures, while also allowing them a glimpse of the fascinating life cycle that many insects undergo. Interacting with living creatures can support children's growth and development in the areas of language, literacy, and social-emotional development. Here are a few ideas for fun and less-intensive pet experiences:

- Collecting caterpillars and watching the transformation to butterflies can be an unforgettable classroom experience. Children will delight in collecting food for caterpillars and can quickly see how much the caterpillars eat. Observing caterpillars offers huge learning opportunities in math (such as measuring the caterpillar, counting the number of leaves eaten, or counting the number of days from chrysalis to butterfly), as well as other study areas, such as social science (studying their migration) and art (diagramming their transformation). Not only do children get to see an amazing example of metamorphosis, but they also have a chance to be scientists by studying and tracking the growth of caterpillars. The transformation from chrysalis to butterfly is nothing short of miraculous! (Again, I discourage educators from mail-ordering caterpillars and releasing them, due to physiological differences and disease transmission between regional ecosystems.)

- You may wish to "adopt" some animals that live outdoors. For example, you could set up a bird-feeding station outside your windows and spend time each day watching the birds visit the feeders and birdbath. Provide food and water consistently. It may take a while before you have lots of birds, but they will come. Learn the names of the birds that visit your feeder. Invest in some easy-to-use field guides, and mark the pages of the book that depict the birds you commonly see. Invite the children to hone their observation skills by drawing the birds they see. It won't be long before your class feels a sense of "ownership" or friendliness toward the birds and eagerly looks forward to watching them and feeding them. (Be aware that many birdseed mixes contain peanuts, which can cause severe allergic reactions in some children. Search for seed mixes that do not contain peanuts or tree nuts.)

- Some classrooms undertake research projects where they count or "survey" the number and kind of birds, butterflies, or dragonflies in a certain area, such as a local park. Returning to an area weekly or seasonally, you can learn about your native species' breeding habits, migration, habitat, and food supply. In many cases, the presence or absence of particular species may tell you something about the environmental health of the area. Such a project may be beyond the realm of some preschool classes, but older children will find it an enjoyable long-term activity that crosses many disciplines and strengthens math, science, and social studies skills. Check appendix A, Additional Resources, for ideas and specific projects.

In some elementary schools, preschools, and churches, it is common practice to incubate chicken or duck eggs with the intention of sending the ducklings and chicks home with children to keep as pets. I strongly discourage this practice. Regardless of the educational opportunities it might present, hatching chicks and ducks for this purpose is unethical because of the extreme stress and hardship on the baby birds. Furthermore, this practice places an undue burden on families who then need to find homes for the birds. The animals may suffer death or injury during transport or from inappropriate living conditions, or as a result of improper care. Children's health may be negatively affected as a result of their close contact with the birds' dander and fecal matter. In some states this practice is illegal.

If you are considering keeping chickens as permanent classroom pets, be sure to carefully, thoroughly research their requirements, needs, and care, and be aware of the associated risks before letting yourself fall in love with the idea of cute chicks hatching in front of the children.

Animal "Coaches" and Visitors

Another way teachers can introduce animals is by partnering with an organization that pairs trained animal reading "coaches" with children. Reading to animals is something that seems natural to children. They love to share their reading abilities with younger children and with animals, and doing so can boost students' reading levels along with their confidence. Many educators capitalize on this interest by hosting classroom visitors for the children to read to. Programs like this allow trained volunteers to bring animal ambassadors (usually dogs, but sometimes cats, rabbits, or even chickens) to the classroom, where children can read to them. Animals offer children a perfect opportunity to practice their academic skills without being corrected, judged, or monitored. There is no pressure to perform; the dog doesn't know if the child is missing a word or two from the story and won't jump in to correct the child when he makes a mistake. When children have the opportunity to practice reading to a dog, cat, or other animal, their proficiency goes up, and their reading skills increase. In addition, many children find their time with a pet to be comforting and almost therapeutic. In one school district, children in kindergarten through grade three had the opportunity to read to dogs once per week for thirty-four weeks. Teachers reported that the children became incredibly attached to the pets and that their fluency and confidence went up. Even occasional visits from an animal "coach" can be beneficial. Some children who struggle with reading are also shy or lack confidence in their social abilities, and dogs can offer a safe way for the children to reach out to others.

Reading to animals can also happen at home with the family pet. Parents should resist the urge to pressure or push children to read to their pets but should be matter-of-fact and gently encouraging when they find their children are interested in reading to the family pet. Just as a dog or other small animal will listen with a nonjudgmental ear in the classroom, at home a friendly pet can provide a child a safe presence in which to practice reading and just have fun. Parents who want to encourage their children to read might suggest story time with the family cat or dog.

Simply the act of petting a dog has been shown to have physiological benefits such as reduced heart rate and lowered blood pressure. Children in stressful situations benefit from the presence of animals. Even college campuses occasionally host therapy dogs during finals week to help quell the nerves and anxiety of students burdened with test pressures.

Educators often involve animals in their classroom to help students with other specific needs. Many children who participate in these programs are on the autism spectrum and are more comfortable connecting and speaking to animals than to people. A body of compelling research suggests that children with autism spectrum disorders who make connections with animals develop a greater sense of comfort and safety with social interactions. In many cases, children on the autism spectrum exhibit a greater comfort

and freedom with pets than with people, and children who spend time with animals show a reduction in hyperactivity symptoms and are better able to concentrate, relax, and follow directions. Some research indicates that children with autism are more social and less prone to self-stimulating behaviors when guided toward engaging with animals. Refer to appendix A, Additional Resources, for a list of organizations that are doing significant work in this area.

Consider bringing animals into the classroom for therapeutic reasons. An animal's presence even for short times in the classroom can be calming for all students. Simply allowing a child to sit quietly with a rat or take a dog for a walk can have a large impact on a child's world. Spending time with an animal can be the difference between a child having a good day, feeling successful in his social interactions, and having a bad day, where he's challenged to calm down, be still, and follow directions. There are countless examples of animals being used to help children overcome emotional barriers, build confidence, and strengthen their relationships with others. Consistent, careful use of animals has been shown to reduce aggression and improve cooperation, increase attention, and improve verbal and social skills. Animals, by virtue of their nonverbal acceptance, are natural partners for many children who are struggling emotionally or physically.

Researcher Aaron Katcher, who for years has studied the use of animals as therapeutic tools for children with attention deficit hyperactivity disorder (ADHD), oppositional defiant disorder, and other disorders, has published some significant findings with regard to animals in therapeutic settings. One study took place at a residential school for children with severe behavioral issues. Bear in mind that the setting was a "zoo" within the residential center, so this example is different from what might take place in a classroom or nature center. Still, the results are compelling and intriguing, and they show that animals can be used effectively to help children in many ways. In Katcher's study, children agreed to take on responsibilities to care for animals' welfare, gradually leading up to adopting animals and even breeding and caring for animals' offspring. With the help of a teacher, the children identified the wants and needs of the animals. This helped the children to feel empathy and practice perspective taking. After thoroughly discussing the wants and needs of the animals, the children were allowed to help care for the animals, feeding and watering them.

Katcher's study also found that animals were effective at holding children's attention. In many cases, "even children with quite limited intelligence or capacity to follow verbal directions persisted in learning the skills and information necessary for them to handle the animals." Children's relationships with the adult instructors in the zoo program improved as well. Within this "classroom zoo" setting, the children wanted to be near to the adults, viewed them as "experts" on the animals, and demonstrated more appropriate social behavior within that context. Children's reported self-impressions were also higher than for children who did not have regular access to the zoo program.

While animals are not a magic "fix-all" for struggling children, you now have an idea of the therapeutic roles animals can play in children's lives for those who are willing to carefully invest in this process. Teachers, psychologists, and others can use animals in deliberate ways to help a variety of children, such as those with behavior issues or ADHD, those on the autism spectrum, those "at-risk" from trouble at home, poverty, or addiction, and those with physical handicaps. Katcher reports a study that found when children with physical disabilities traveled in wheelchairs in the presence of their service dogs, they received ten times as much attention and social interaction as when they were without their dogs. This finding has important implications for combating potential isolation and depression in children with physical disabilities. Although not all classrooms allow animals such as dogs, educators can recognize the importance of animals in breaking down barriers for children who may feel isolated and disconnected due to physical or mental disabilities.

Again, animals can break down barriers, remove obstacles, provide a safe sounding board for children, and offer unconditional love and acceptance to children. Animals can serve as "connectors" for bringing children together socially and help children who may be feeling lost or isolated. And animals in the classroom can help with learning in more direct ways, too. There are many programs that use teams of dogs and volunteers to help children practice academic skills. Check appendix A, Additional Resources, for information on how you can be paired with a team or host a visitor to your classroom. You can involve animals in your classroom in a variety of ways to support all children's learning.

A classroom pet can enrich the lives of children in many ways. Pets in the classroom can help children learn about and practice caregiving, develop responsibility and self-confidence, and even encourage social interactions between children. Animals in the classroom help children learn self-regulation and perspective taking. They offer children ways to connect emotionally with each other through shared interests and shared responsibility. Finally, animals in the classroom offer teachers connections to all curricular disciplines. And children's inherent interest in animals means that animals can help boost learning! Animals are special friends to children and hold a special place in the hearts of many, and for good reason.

From providing opportunities to show genuine care, to offering comfort dealing with intense feelings, to piquing a child's curiosity and learning, I hope this book has shown you that animals can be a welcome addition to the classroom. With careful planning, a strong commitment, and clear outcomes and objectives, you can enhance children's learning, their relationships, and their experiences by including animals in their lives. As you move forward with your plans, please know that you have my best wishes and support. Avail yourself of the resources in your area, from your county extension office to local enthusiasts clubs to volunteer organizations. You'll find there is no shortage of people interested in helping you help children build lasting bonds with animals that will enrich their learning throughout their lives.

Appendix A
Additional Resources

Alliance for Childhood publishes resources aimed at those who work and play with young children, including many resources for educators. www.allianceforchildhood.org

American Academy of Pediatrics' website contains resources and information about children's health. It also includes links to position papers on screen time, children's health, and more. www.aap.org

Association of Zoos and Aquariums' website, although mostly for professionals in the industry, offers news and articles pertaining to animals in zoos and aquariums, as well as conservation and education resources. www.aza.org

The Center for Place-Based Education at Antioch University New England (formerly the Center for Environmental Education) promotes community-based education programs. www.antiochne.edu/anei/cpbe

The Cornell Lab of Ornithology is a nonprofit organization at Cornell University with a host of resources for studying and appreciating birds. Cornell University also maintains a searchable database of a myriad of citizen science projects, many of which involve animals and are great for educators. www.birds.cornell.edu and www.birds.cornell.edu/citsci

Green Chimneys is a multifaceted nonprofit organization helping young people to maximize their full potential by providing residential, educational, clinical, and recreational services that create and nurture connections to the community and the natural world. They are one of the first child-animal therapy organizations and a great resource. www.greenchimneys.org

Healthy Pets, Healthy People is a website of the Centers for Disease Control and Prevention. It's full of information and news about pets, health-related issues related to animals, and more. www.cdc.gov/healthypets

The Institute for Humane Education aims to "create a just, humane, and sustainable world through education." www.humaneeducation.org

Jane Goodall's Roots & Shoots is a global environmental education program for youth. (http://www.rootsandshoots.org). One result of the program is a book titled *Kids & Animals: Drawings from the Hands and Hearts of Children & Youth*.

Mail ordering insects: I don't recommend any sources for mail ordering insects at this time.

Monarch Larva Monitoring Project is a citizen science venture that involves tracking monarch eggs, caterpillars, and pupae through the University of Minnesota. www.mlmp.org

National Association for the Education of Young Children (www.naeyc .org) is a resource for early care and education professionals, and produces guidelines for young children's health and education, such as this position statement on children's media consumption, created jointly with the Fred Rogers Institute: http://www.naeyc.org/files/naeyc/file/positions/Key Messages_Technology.pdf

National Science Teachers Association offers resources and support for teachers of science and teachers who want to teach science topics in the classroom. It also contains links to state and national science standards, as well an official position statement on the use of animals in the classroom. www.nsta.org

Petfinder is an online resource for people looking to adopt a pet. www.pet finder.com

Pet Partners (formerly the Delta Society) aims to connect people and animals, and their website hosts lots of resources on therapy animals, animals in education and service, and project ideas for teachers and children. www .petpartners.org

Promise of Place is a collaborative website on the topic of place-based education and has information including curriculum and planning aids and other resources. www.promiseofplace.org

Classroom Pet Care Checklist

Before you embark on the journey of life with a classroom pet, you should take into account a number of issues. Below is a checklist of some of the major topics to think about. I am not a veterinarian, and this list certainly does not address every detail you need to consider. There is no substitution for real human interaction, so seek out local resources at animal shelters, local rescue clubs, veterinary clinics, and libraries. You'll find lots of people are willing to help you learn more about obtaining a classroom pet!

Discuss your plans with your colleagues, supervisor, director, and others with whom you work.

- What are some ways you can include them in your plans?

- Do they have fears or preferences you need to consider?

- Do they have any concerns about getting an animal?

Learn the rules.

- Are there regulations about what pets you can legally possess in your classroom?

- Talk with others in the field and your accreditation coach or mentor, if you have one. Licensing experts can be helpful also.

Consider *why* you want a pet.

- Have you identified learning outcomes, behavioral changes, or other benefits you're hoping will result?

- What do you see as some benefits of having a class pet?

Consider your own commitment, abilities, and time. Even after the initial excitement of obtaining your pet wears off, it will still need constant care. That takes time.

- What kind of time commitment will this pet take per day, week, month, and year?
- If the pet becomes ill, where will it go while it undergoes care with a vet? (Ill animals should not be in the classroom.)
- Who will be in charge of feeding and watering the animal and cleaning its housing?
- What will happen if you change jobs?
- Who will be the caregiver for the animal during the summer and on long breaks during the school year?

Consider the unique characteristics of the species you are interested in. In addition to many species-specific questions, consider the following:

- Is it nocturnal (active only at night)?
- Is it loud or quiet?
- Does the animal become skittish when disturbed?
- Does the animal do best as a single pet, or will it be happier as half of a pair?
- Can the animal be handled safely by young children?

Consider the unique health needs of the species you are interested in.

- What are its needs for food and water? Does the animal eat fresh food or need prepared food?
- What kind of diet does it have? Does the animal eat live food such as crickets, worms, or mice? If so, are you comfortable with that?
- What are its exercise and physical stimulation needs? Does it need to climb, burrow, hop, or dig?
- Will the animal roam freely in the classroom (not recommended in most settings)?

- Does the animal have a need for direct sunlight? If so, how will you provide access for the animal?

- How will you provide your pet with a shelter where it can retreat when the action in the classroom becomes too intense?

Consider your pet's habitat requirements.

- Will you be getting an aquarium for fish or other aquatic creatures? If so, you'll need a heater, filter, light, thermometer, and more. Other pets such as reptiles require special types of lights and heat sources.

- Will your animal require a specific environment? Some animals will crawl out of cages or tanks without covers. Other animals require certain ambient temperatures or humidity levels.

- If your pet requires bedding material, how frequently does it need to be changed? How will you keep the pet's quarters clean and sanitary?

- Are there any special supplies needed for cleaning the animal's home?

Assess your setting. What's your program like?

- Does it meet year-round or just during the school year?

- Is your classroom relatively loud and active, or more quiet and subdued?

- Are the children of mixed ages?

- How big is your class?

- Do you own or lease the space where you are located? (In some cases, leases may preclude you from having a pet. Do your homework.)

- Do you have access to outdoor spaces where your pet may roam safely in the sunshine?

Identify your logistical needs.

- Where will the pet be housed? Find a location in the classroom that is accessible but not smack in the middle of the action.

- Where will you store your pet's supplies, such as bedding, food, supplements (if needed), and cleaning supplies (that are exclusive for your pet's care)?

Know your budget.

- Besides the initial cost of the animal and its habitat requirements, how will you plan for an ongoing supply of food, bedding, and vitamin supplements (if necessary)?

- Do you have a budget for toys and equipment for enrichment (such as things to chew on, climb on)?

- How much will medical care cost *for the life of the animal*? Start a fund or have a budget for emergency medical expenses that may arise.

Research your animal's "normal."

- What does "healthy" look like for your animal? Be aware of any behavioral or physical changes that may indicate that the animal is ill, under stress, or otherwise compromised. If this occurs, be prepared to remove the animal from the classroom, and work with your vet immediately to provide care for your pet.

Engage the children in planning and researching prospective pets.

- Create a list of ideas, and evaluate them together. If appropriate for the age group, conduct research.

- What roles will the children have in caring for your pet? Create a list of all the things they can do to help care for the pet.

- As early as possible, establish guidelines about handling the pet, how frequently the children have direct access to the animal, and other issues around direct interaction. Be sure everyone understands the rules. Revisit them as your needs and the animal's needs change.

Know your resources and support.

- What local animal shelters, veterinarians, enthusiasts clubs, or pet rescue organizations are available for you to partner with? Find experts and others with experience to help you learn more, and on whom you can lean if you need help once you have the pet.

• Are there veterinarians who will commit to helping you care for the animal? Are there parents in your school community who have a pet of your preferred species who can offer advice and suggestions?

Have a plan. It is imperative that there be a backup caregiver (or two, or three!) in the event that you are ill, traveling, or unavailable. Be certain you have a plan in place for care for the animal throughout its life, regardless of the circumstances in your classroom.

Appendix C

References

meaningful encounters with animals Kidd, Aline H., and Robert M. Kidd. 1990. "Social and Environmental Influences on Children's Attitudes Toward Pets." *Psychological Reports* 67:807–18.

exclude humans from their definitions Herrmann, Patricia A., Douglas L. Medin, and Sandra R. Waxman. 2012. "When Humans Become Animals: Development of the Animal Category in Early Childhood." *Cognition* 122 (1): 74–79. doi:10.1016/j.cognition.2011.08.011.

animals in the care of humans n.d. Association of Zoos and Aquariums. Phone call with the author.

biophilia hypothesis Wilson, Edward. 1984. *Biophilia: The Human Bond with Other Species*. Cambridge, MA: Harvard University Press.

children's academic growth, behavior, and stress levels Kellert, Stephen R. 2005. *Building for Life: Designing and Understanding the Human-Nature Connection*. Washington, DC: Island Press.

disliking animals is simply "wrong," Kidd, Aline H., and Robert M. Kidd. 1990. "Social and Environmental Influences on Children's Attitudes Toward Pets." *Psychological Reports* 67:807–18.

multiple intelligences Gardner, Howard. 2011. *Frames of Mind: The Theory of Multiple Intelligences*. New York: Basic Books.

positively affect children's learning Kellert, Stephen R. 2005. *Building for Life: Designing and Understanding the Human-Nature Connection*. Washington, DC: Island Press.

"nonhuman others" Myers, Gene. 2007. *The Significance of Children and Animals: Social Development and Our Connections to Other Species*. 2nd, revised edition. West Lafayette, IN: Purdue University Press.

"human mind is especially good at mirroring" Myers, Gene. 2012. Email message to author. December 4.

children use agency and affect as keys Ibid.

"net effect of such repeated interactions" Ibid.

a common language Blue, Gladys F. 1986. "The Value of Pets in Children's Lives." *Childhood Education* 63 (2): 85–90.

animal behaviorists Bekoff, Marc. 2010. *The Animal Manifesto: Six Reasons for Expanding Our Compassion Footprint.* Novato, CA: New World Library.

Young children assume Myers, Gene. 2007. *The Significance of Children and Animals: Social Development and Our Connections to Other Species.* 2nd, revised edition. West Lafayette, IN: Purdue University.

thinking about that child Triebenbacher, Sandra Lookabaugh. 1998. "Pets as Transitional Objects: Their Role in Children's Emotional Development." *Psychological Reports* 82 (1): 191–200. doi: 10.2466/pr0.1998.82.1.191.

attunement Lasher, Margot. 1998. "A Relational Approach to The Human-Animal Bond." *Anthrozoös: A Multidisciplinary Journal of the Interactions of People & Animals* 11 (3): 130–133. doi: 10.2752/089279398787000670.

the child perceives the animal as communicating Ibid.

crucial experiences Kellert, Stephen R. 2005. *Building for Life: Designing and Understanding the Human-Nature Connection.* Washington, DC: Island Press.

lifelong influence Myers, Gene. 2007. *The Significance of Children and Animals: Social Development and Our Connections to Other Species.* 2nd, revised edition. West Lafayette, IN: Purdue University Press.

transitional objects Winnicott, Donald Woods. 1953. "Transitional Objects and Transitional Phenomena—A Study of the First Not-Me Possession." *International Journal of Psycho-Analysis* 34:89–97.

individuation Mahler, Margaret S., Fred Pine, and Anni Bergman. 1975. *The Psychological Birth of the Human Infant: Symbiosis and Individuation.* New York: Basic Books.

positive early experiences a child has with animals Kidd, Aline H., and Robert M. Kidd. 1990. "Social and Environmental Influences on Children's Attitudes Toward Pets." *Psychological Reports* 67:807–18.

even very young children have a solid grasp of what animals need Myers, Olin E., Jr., Carol D. Saunders, and Erik Garrett. 2004. "What Do Children Think Animals Need?: Developmental Trends." *Environmental Education Research* 10 (4): 545–62. doi: 10.1080/1350462042000291056.

can grow into feelings of stewardship Kidd, Aline H., and Robert M. Kidd. 1990. "Social and Environmental Influences on Children's Attitudes Toward Pets." *Psychological Reports* 67:807–18.

three elements of caregiving Myers, Olin Eugene, Jr., and Carol D. Saunders. 2002. "Animals as Links toward Developing Caring Relationships with the Natural World." In *Children and Nature: Psychological, Sociocultural, and Evolutionary Investigations*, edited by Peter H. Kahn Jr. and Stephen R. Kellert, 153–78. Cambridge, MA: Massachusetts Institute of Technology.

boys are socially conditioned against being caregivers Melson, Gail F. 2001. *Why the Wild Things Are: Animals in the Lives of Children*. Cambridge, MA: Harvard University Press.

Researchers showed the children line drawings Ibid.

Toys traditionally associated with caregiving and housekeeping Rheingold, Harriet L., and Kaye V. Cook. 1975. "The Contents of Boys' and Girls' Rooms as an Index of Parents' Behavior." *Child Development* 46 (2): 459–63. http://www.jstor.org/stable/1128142.

competence in cooperation Kotrschal, Kurt, and Brita Ortbauer. 2003. "Behavioral Effects of the Presence of a Dog in a Classroom." *Anthrozoös: A Multidisciplinary Journal of the Interactions of People & Animals* 16 (3): 147–59.

with exposure children become "cognizant . . ." Kellert, Stephen R. 2002. "Experiencing Nature: Affective, Cognitive, and Evaluative Development in Children." In *Children and Nature: Psychological, Sociocultural, and Evolutionary Investigations*, edited by Peter H. Kahn Jr. and Stephen R. Kellert, 133. Cambridge, MA: Massachusetts Institute of Technology.

One study looked at young children's attitudes Triebenbacher, Sandra Lookabaugh. 1998. "Pets as Transitional Objects: Their Role in Children's Emotional Development" *Psychological Reports* 82 (1): 191–200. doi: 10.2466/pr0.1998.82.1.191.

strong attachment bonds between children and animals Daly, Beth, and L. L. Morton. 2006. "An Investigation of Human-Animal Interactions as

Related to Pet Preference, Ownership, Attachment, and Attitudes in Children." *Anthrozoös: A Multidisciplinary Journal of the Interactions of People & Animals* 19 (2): 113–27. doi: 10.2752/089279306785593801.

relationship has the quality of attunement Lasher, Margot. 1998. "A Relational Approach to the Human-Animal Bond." *Anthrozoös: A Multidisciplinary Journal of the Interactions of People & Animals* 11 (3): 130–33. doi: 10.2752/089279398787000670.

Children's attachment to companion animals can also Katcher, Aaron. 2002. "Animals in Therapeutic Education: Guides into the Liminal State." In *Children and Nature: Psychological, Sociocultural, and Evolutionary Investigations,* edited by Peter H. Kahn Jr. and Stephen R. Kellert, 179–98. Cambridge, MA: Massachusetts Institute of Technology.

The act of petting an animal has been shown to lower blood pressure Beck, Alan M., and N. Marshall Meyers. 1996. "Health Enhancement and Companion Animal Ownership." *Annual Review of Public Health* 17:247–57. doi: 10.1146/annurev.pu.17.050196.001335.

Empathy is defined as "understanding, being aware of . . ." "Empathy." 2013. Merriam-Webster.com. Accessed September 23. http://www.merriam-webster.com/dictionary/empathy.

When children have empathy for animals, they also feel more empathy Poresky, Robert H. 1990. "The Young Children's Empathy Measure: Reliability, Validity And Effects of Companion Animal Bonding." *Psychological Reports* 66:931–36. doi: 10.2466/pr0.1990.66.3.931.

children apply their newly developing sense of justice Gilligan, Carol, and Grant Wiggins. 1987. "The Origins of Morality in Early Childhood Relationships." In *The Emergence of Morality in Young Children*, edited by Jerome Kagan and Sharon Lamb, 277–305. Chicago: University of Chicago Press.

see it as "highly probable" Myers, Olin Eugene, Jr., and Carol D. Saunders. 2002. "Animals as Links toward Developing Caring Relationships with the Natural World." In *Children and Nature: Psychological, Sociocultural, and Evolutionary Investigations*, edited by Peter H. Kahn Jr. and Stephen R. Kellert, 153–78. Cambridge, MA: Massachusetts Institute of Technology.

as children's cognitive understanding of animals' . . . grows Ibid.

In 2012, the total amount spent on pets . . . Over 62 percent of households American Pet Products Association. 2013. "U.S. Pet Industry Spending Figures and Future Outlook." Accessed June 12. http://www.americanpet products.org/press_industrytrends.asp.

children from homes with pets typically show more empathy Poresky, Robert H. 1990. "The Young Children's Empathy Measure: Reliability, Validity and Effects of Companion Animal Bonding." *Psychological Reports* 66:931–36. doi: 10.2466/pr0.1990.66.3.931.

In the wake of the tragic effects of Hurricane Katrina in 2005 DiBlasio, Natalie. 2012. "Hurricane Katrina's 'Silver Lining': Improved Pet Care." *USA Today,* last modified August 31. http://usatoday30.usatoday.com/weather /storms/story/2012-08-30/Isaac-pets-emergency-plan-Katrina/57454202/1.

Pet Evacuation and Transportation Standards Act of 2006 Pets Evacuation and Transportation Standards Act of 2006. http://www.govtrack.us /congress/bills/109/hr3858.

Parents' language patterns . . . even provoking fears or phobias in children Muris, Peter, Lisanne van Zwol, Jorg Huijding, and Birgit Mayer. 2010. "Mom Told Me Scary Things About This Animal: Parents Installing Fear Beliefs in Their Children via the Verbal Information Pathway." *Behavior Research and Therapy* 48 (4): 341–46. doi: 10.1016/j.brat.2009.12.001.

children can identify with these generic similarities Karniol, Rachel. 2012. "Storybook-Induced Arousal and Preschoolers' Empathetic Understanding of Negative Affect in Self, Others, and Animals in Stories." *Journal of Research in Childhood Education* 26:346–58. doi: 10.1080/02568543.2012684423.

over one thousand fiction and nonfiction children's books Marriott, Stuart. 2002. "Red in Tooth and Claw? Images of Nature in Modern Picture Books." *Children's Literature in Education* 33 (3): 175–83.

estimates the total television time for children under age eleven Nielsen. 2011. *Television Audience Report 2010–2011.* http://www.nielsen.com/us/en /reports/2011/television-audience-report-2010-2011.html.

reports that by age three, about one-third of American children American Academy of Pediatrics. 2011. "Media Use by Children Younger Than 2 Years." *Pediatrics* 128:1040–44. doi: 10.1542/peds.2011-1753

Children may see themselves mirrored in characters Burke, Carolyn L., and Joby G. Copenhaver. 2004. "Animals as People in Children's Literature." *Language Arts* 81 (3): 205–13. http://www.ncte.org/library/nctefiles/store/samplefiles/journals/la/la0813animals.pdf.

It is actually easier for the child to identify with the character Karniol, Rachel. 2012. "Storybook-Induced Arousal and Preschoolers' Empathetic Understanding of Negative Affect in Self, Others, and Animals in Stories." *Journal of Research in Childhood Education* 26:346–58. doi: 10.1080/02568 543.2012.684423.

project their own feelings and "inner struggles" onto the animal characters Burke, Carolyn L., and Joby G. Copenhaver. 2004. "Animals as People in Children's Literature." *Language Arts* 81 (3): 205–13. http://www.ncte.org/library/nctefiles/store/samplefiles/journals/la/la0813animals.pdf.

fairy tales the world over: animals can be Bettelheim, Bruno. 2010. *The Uses of Enchantment: The Meaning and Importance of Fairy Tales*. New York: Vintage Books.

"Hero's Journey" Campbell, Joseph. 1949. *The Hero With a Thousand Faces*. New York: Pantheon Books.

most educators, pediatricians, and child development experts agree: children do respond to the subtle messages Campaign for a Commercial-Free Childhood, Alliance for Childhood, and Teachers Resisting Unhealthy Children's Entertainment. 2012. *Facing the Screen Dilemma: Young Children, Technology and Early Education*. Boston, MA: Campaign for a Commercial-Free Childhood. www.commercialfreechildhood.org/sites/default/files/facingthescreendilemma.pdf.

encountering wild animals ignite a spark of curiosity Kellert, Stephen R. 2002. "Experiencing Nature: Affective, Cognitive, and Evaluative Development in Children." In *Children and Nature: Psychological, Sociocultural, and Evolutionary Investigations* edited by Peter H. Kahn Jr. and Stephen R. Kellert. Cambridge, MA: Massachusetts Institute of Technology.

that love expands and is generalized to other living creatures Chawla, Louise. 1999. "Life Paths into Effective Environmental Action." *The Journal of Environmental Education* 31 (1): 15–26. doi: 10.1080/00958969909598628.

Place-based education can be done any time, anywhere Lieberman, Gerald A., and Linda L. Hoody. 1998. "Closing the Achievement Gap: Using the Environment as an Integrating Context for Learning." State Education and Environment Roundtable. Ponway, CA: Science Wizards. http://www.seer.org/extras/execsum.pdf.

children need to have an intimate knowledge of familiar animals Sobel, David. 1996. *Beyond Ecophobia: Reclaiming the Heart in Nature Education.* Great Barrington, MA: Orion Society.

the special zoo just for young children Chicago Zoological Society. 2013. "Hamill Family Play Zoo." Accessed September 14. http://www.czs.org/CZS/playzoo.

freedom to "become" animals can be a powerful way to support children's Sobel, David. 1996. *Beyond Ecophobia: Reclaiming the Heart in Nature Education.* Great Barrington, MA: Orion Society.

creative opportunity "to put their own ideas into action . . ." Bekoff, Marc. n.d. Email message to author.

participation of an enthusiastic adult Chawla, Louise. 1999. "Life Paths into Effective Environmental Action." *The Journal of Environmental Education* 31 (1): 15–26. doi: 10.1080/00958969909598628.

animals in the classroom expands learning opportunities for children Daly, Beth, and Suzanne Suggs. 2010. "Teachers' Experiences with Humane Education and Animals in the Elementary Classroom: Implications for Empathy Development." *Journal of Moral Education* 39 (1): 101–12. doi: 10.1080/03057240903528733.

the common brown earthworm . . . is not native to many parts of North America Bohlen, Patrick J., Stefan Scheu, Cindy M. Hale, Mary Ann McLean, Sonja Migge, Peter M. Groffman, and Dennis Parkinson. 2004. "Non-Native Invasive Earthworms as Agents of Change in Northern Temperate Forests." *Frontiers in Ecology and the Environment* 2 (8): 427–35.

discourages children under five from handling reptiles or birds Centers for Disease Control. 2012. "*Salmonella* Infection (salmonellosis) and Animals." Last modified August 7. http://www.cdc.gov/healthypets/diseases/salmonellosis.htm.

asthma triggers for children with allergies to animal dander Smith, Kristine M., Katherine F. Smith, and Jennifer P. D'Auria. 2012. "Exotic Pets: Health and Safety Issues for Children and Parents." *Journal of Pediatric Health Care* 26 (2): e2–e6. doi:10.1016/j.pedhc.2011.11.009.

rate of childhood asthma continues to rise Goodman, David C., Therese A. Stukel, and Chiang-hua Chang. 1998. "Trends in Pediatric Asthma Hospitalization Rates: Regional and Socioeconomic Differences." *Pediatrics* 101 (2): 208–13. doi: 10.1542/peds.101.2.208.

boost students' reading levels along with their confidence Jalongo, Mary Renck. 2005. "What Are All These Dogs Doing at School?": Using Therapy Dogs to Promote Children's Reading Practice." *Childhood Education* 81 (3): 152–58. doi: 10.1080/00094056.2005.10522259.

In one school district . . . Teachers reported that . . . fluency and confidence went up Tales of Joy R.E.A.D. Program. 2013. "Annual Data Report." http://www.therapyanimals.org/Research_%26_Results.html

reduced heart rate and lowered blood pressure Beck, Alan M., and N. Marshall Meyers. 1996. "Health Enhancement and Companion Animal Ownership." *Annual Review Public Health* 17:247–57. doi: 10.1146/annurev.pu.17.050196.001335.

children with autism spectrum disorders who make connections with animals Friesen, Lori. 2010. "Exploring Animal-Assisted Programs with Children in School and Therapeutic Contexts." *Early Childhood Education Journal* 37 (4): 261–67. doi: 10.1007/s10643-009-0349-5.

a reduction in hyperactivity symptoms and are better able to concentrate, relax, and follow directions Ibid.

children with autism are more social and less prone to self-stimulating behaviors Redefer, Laurel A., and Joan F. Goodman. 1989. "Brief Report: Pet-Facilitated Therapy With Autistic Children." *Journal of Autism and Developmental Disorders* 19 (3): 461–67. http://autivisie.nl/images/stories/AAT_bij_ASS_1989.pdf.

reduce aggression and improve cooperation Katcher, Aaron. 2002. "Animals in Therapeutic Education: Guides into the Liminal State." In *Children and Nature: Psychological, Sociocultural, and Evolutionary Investigations,* edited by Peter H. Kahn Jr. and Stephen R. Kellert, 179–98. Cambridge, MA: Massachusetts Institute of Technology.

"even children with quite limited intelligence" Ibid. 184.

the children . . . demonstrated more appropriate social behavior within that context Ibid.

when children with physical disabilities traveled in wheelchairs Ibid.

Index

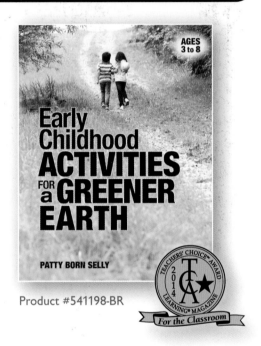